FOOD ESSENTIALS

GRAINS AND PASTA

FOOD ESSENTIALS

GRAINS AND PASTA

BY CAROL SPIER

PHOTOGRAPHY BY BILL MILNE

Friedman Group

A FRIEDMAN GROUP BOOK

ISBN 0-517-06117-1

FOOD ESSENTIALS: GRAINS AND PASTA
was prepared and produced by
Michael Friedman Publishing Group, Inc.
15 West 26th Street
New York, New York 10010

Editor: Nathaniel Marunas
Art Director: Jeff Batzli
Layout: Susan Livingston
Photography Editor: Christopher C. Bain
Production: Jeanne E. Kaufman

Typeset by Trufont Typographers, Inc.
Color separations by Rainbow Graphic Arts Ltd.
Printed and bound in Hong Kong by Leefung-Asco Printers Ltd.

 **TABLE OF CONTENTS**

DEDICATION

I don't suppose this book would have been possible if I had not once shared a house with Leslie, Steve, and Meg; wherever those lovers of brown rice may be, I would like to think that this book will find its way into their kitchens.

My husband has said he does not expect to see his name on this page, but without his appetite, his tolerance for flying flour, and his true liking for triticale (not to mention his foresight in computer acquisition) this book would not be.

ACKNOWLEDGMENTS

There was a time when I dropped all meat from my diet and learned to make meals from rice, wheat, and millet. Though I am no longer a strict vegetarian, these wonderful foods have held since that time a prominent place in my cuisine, where they mix effortlessly with the fresh, light, and simple foods I prefer to eat. So it was with delight that I agreed to write this book when Karla Olson, loveliest of editors, offered me the opportunity.

Many fine cooks and knowledgeable writers have preceded me in creating cookbooks, and as I researched this volume I inevitably incurred a debt to them that must be noted. To all the wonderful authors and publishers who have brought myriad inspiring (and grain-intensive) ethnic cuisines to bookshelves, my thanks. And to Marlene Anne Bumgarner, Irma S. Rombauer and Marion Rombauer Becker, and Jane E. Brody, my gratitude for making the essentials of grains, cooking, and nutrition so accessible.

PREFACE

There are those people who are natural cooks, and those who quake at the idea of preparing anything more complex than scrambled eggs on toast. The former tend to be creative in the kitchen, and are always on the lookout for both new ideas and basic culinary knowledge that will allow them to follow a whim with a certain guarantee of success; the latter rarely reach beyond the tried-and-true without a cookbook in hand. The former may eschew measuring spoons in favor of "season to taste," while the latter ponder level versus heaping. Both will find guidance and inspiration in the *Food Essentials* series.

Topically organized, these volumes contain the basics of food preparation in an accessible and straightforward format.

But they are much more than convenient, alphabetized indexes of what-is-it-called and how-do-you-cook-it. The *Food Essentials* volumes address all of the culinary needs of today's cook, explaining not only the elemental aspects of buying, storage, and preparation, but the nutritional role played by each of the various foods. The contemporary attitude expressed throughout is one of good health through good food with as little trouble as possible; the diversity of the recipes is unified by common-sense nutrition, fresh ingredients simply but delightfully seasoned, and ease of preparation. The text is sprinkled with bits of food history and countless suggestions for seasoning variations. Both timid and adventurous cooks will be rewarded with every reading of these essential volumes.

There is probably no food category as versatile *and* nutritious as grains. By definition the seeds of certain grass plants, these small, dry bits—whether you call them groats, berries, kernels, grains, or seeds—can be seasoned in infinite ways, used whole or ground into flour, and placed in every part of the menu. They provide us with many essential nutrients, and they are inexpensive, long-lived in the larder, and easy and fairly quick to prepare.

Grains, particularly when eaten in their less-refined forms, are high in protein, fiber, vitamins, and minerals. Although their protein is not complete (it lacks some of the essential amino acids), when eaten in combination with other foods (certain vegetables, legumes, and dairy products), they can take the place of meat in our diet. And because they are carbohydrates, they provide our bodies with energy. They are also very tasty, and take almost any kind of seasoning.

The very versatility of grains made the creation of this book an unusual challenge. So many little dried pieces, each with a unique taste that worked to advantage in particular recipes but seemed to work just as well in all the other recipes. So much brown, white, and beige, such a tendency to make dry or globby mounds on the plate. All that nutritional value to be taken advantage of, but how to make it appealing, how to keep it from resembling the heavy cuisine so often associated with health foods, how not to negate its natural goodness with rich or salty sauces? And how to fit all this terrific information in one book?

Once the grains were identified and their general history and culinary flavors described, it was, of course, essential to explain how to cook them in their commonly found forms. Then it was important to provide recipes that are traditionally associated with specific grains—polenta with corn, Scotch broth with barley, couscous with millet, rice pudding with rice. Each of the grains deserved to be used in a variety of ways as well—in pilafs, soups, salads, and desserts—and cooked with the most enhancing seasonings. An effort was made to create entrées and recipes that could serve as main *or* side dishes. An effort was made to create meatless recipes, although some

meat, poultry, and seafood begged to be included. The recipes needed to rely not upon cream, eggs, or cheese for flavor or substance, but upon the grains themselves. And they had to be fairly easy to prepare, using ingredients that were readily available, or few people would bother to make them.

A few wonderful things came to light as this book was put together. The first was the discovery that many of the less-familiar grains have exquisite flavors and can be steamed and enjoyed on their own, or served simply with butter, yogurt, or soy sauce. Then there is hardly a cuisine in the world that does not take advantage of grains. The seasonings appropriate for inclusion were unlimited, and though specific grains were complemented particularly by certain seasonings, most of the grains were enhanced by others, too, and were delicious sweet, savory, or spicy. Perhaps the best discovery of all was the many different flours with their unusual flavors that work to great advantage in cookies, pancakes, muffins, and quick breads.

So by way of instruction in the use of this book, there is one key word—experiment. Buy the grains you've never heard of—take a stroll down the exotic-food aisle of your supermarket or visit your local health-food store (you may be surprised by the sophistication of both). Follow the recipes here as they are written, but don't hesitate to be creative: If you allow for the disparities in their cooking times, many of the grains can be substituted for one another with great success, and many of the recipes can be followed for method but reflavored by commonsense substitution of spices or herbs.

In recipes that call for butter, use sweet or lightly salted, whichever you prefer. Broth can be made from vegetable, chicken, or beef stock, according to your dietary needs. Just remember that the flavor of the particular stock you use will affect the taste of the prepared food.

Amaranth, barley, buckwheat, corn, millet, oats, quinoa, rice, rye, triticale, wheat—some familiar names and others exotic-sounding new ones. Try each one and you will take a gustatory journey with scenery as lovely as that on a relaxed country stroll—not breathtaking but filled with bits of natural wonder.

Amaranth (from the Greek for "never-fading flower") is an annual herb, and is therefore not a true grain. It has broad leaves and large flower heads that produce thousands of tiny, protein-rich seeds. There are hundreds of varieties of amaranth. It is grown for its leaves—some varieties are good in salad, some are delicious steamed or stir-fried—and its somewhat peppery seeds. (The garden flower globe amaranth is not related.)

Amaranth is believed to have been a staple in the diet of pre-Columbian Aztecs, who thought that it gave them supernatural powers and incorporated it into their religious ceremonies. After conquering Montezuma in 1519, the Spanish forbade its use and amaranth has been introduced only recently to contemporary cuisine.

Amaranth is a relative of pigweed, the common wild plant also known as lamb's-quarters. Like pigweed, it is a vigorous and nutrient-rich plant. For a grain, amaranth is unusually high in protein (15 to 18 percent), and contains lysine and methionine, two essential amino acids that are not often found in this food group. It is high in fiber and contains calcium, iron, and vitamins A and C. Because it is both nutritious and very adaptive to adverse growing conditions, there is a great deal of research being done on amaranth; it is likely that it will become a familiar food very soon.

Amaranth can be cooked as a cereal. The seeds are very tiny—looking a bit

Amaranth bears a cascade of blooms that yield a profusion of tiny, nutritious seeds.

like caviar when cooked—and their lack of substance makes them rather unsatisfactory as the base of pilaf-type dishes. Amaranth is often ground into flour and used with equal success in sweet or savory baked goods. There is a hint of vegetable flavor in amaranth, and it is particularly complemented by yogurt (with or without honey), sharp herbs such as coriander, and curry-type dishes.

You are not likely to find amaranth on the shelves of every grocery, but health-food stores stock both whole amaranth seeds and amaranth flour; they may also carry packaged amaranth products such as cereals and pasta.

WHAT TO LOOK FOR IN THE MARKET

Whole Amaranth Seeds

Whole Amaranth Seeds

Amaranth seeds are tiny, golden, and round. They can be sprouted, popped, toasted, or cooked to make cereal. You can use them as you would sesame seeds, to top breads or add flavor and crunch to cookies; cooked, they can be added to stir-fries or used to dredge poultry or fish. You can also add them to the water in which you are steaming a larger grain when about ten minutes of cooking time remains; fluff the two together with a fork to mix before serving. Amaranth cooks very quickly, so it is a good choice for a quick, nutritious hot porridge.

Flour

Amaranth flour has a fairly strong malt-like vegetable taste and is beige in color. It is an excellent choice for use in any baked goods that will accompany well-seasoned vegetable dishes such as curries or other spicy soups or stews. Substitute it for up to half the all-purpose flour in recipes for biscuits, crepes, or crust for savory pies, or take advantage of its malty flavor and use it to make cookies. You can include it in mixed-grain breads, but it does not contain the necessary gluten to be the primary flour in yeast-raised recipes.

AMARANTH RECIPES

Basic Steamed Amaranth

Amaranth doubles in volume when steamed.

The exact proportion of water to grain and the length of the cooking time will vary somewhat in each individual kitchen—the size and weight of the pan, the intensity of the flame, and the desired degree of softness all influence the results. The directions that follow are for grains that are cooked but discrete; if you wish to make a creamy porridge, increase both the amount of water and the cooking time.

Steamed amaranth is always rather sticky; it makes an excellent hot cereal.

Place 1 part amaranth and 2 parts water in a saucepan. Bring to a boil, cover, reduce the heat and simmer for 15 to 20 minutes. Check after 12 minutes to see that the water has not steamed off before the amaranth is done; if it has, add a bit more water (preferably boiling).

Fluff the cooked amaranth with a fork and serve with butter, yogurt, or soy sauce, or use in recipes calling for cooked whole amaranth.

Basic Popped Amaranth

Amaranth triples in volume when popped.

Amaranth must be popped in very small batches or it will stick to the pan and burn.

Heat a dry heavy skillet over high heat. Stir in just 1 tablespoon of whole amaranth grains. Continue to stir until most of them have popped open; they will not all pop. Transfer the grains to a dish and keep warm. Repeat until desired amount is popped.

Amaranth Crepes with Spinach and Leek Filling

These nutty-flavored crepes are rolled up over mildly spiced spinach and served with a lemony yogurt sauce. The crepes, filling, and sauce can be prepared ahead and refrigerated separately for a few hours before you assemble and bake them. If you do this, be sure to drain any liquid from the filling before assembling the crepes.

The crepes will be most successful if you allow the batter to rest in the refrigerator for 2 to 3 hours (or overnight) before you cook them. They are cooked on only 1 side before they are filled. You will need a crepe pan or an 8-inch frying pan that heats evenly, a small, flexible spatula, and a damp dish towel. Expect the first couple of crepes to be experimental as you find the correct temperature for the pan. If you wish to serve this dish as an appetizer, make the crepes in a smaller frying pan.

You will need at least 1 pint of yogurt to make this dish. Plan to use more if you like to be generous with sauce.

For the crepes:

½	cup amaranth flour
½	cup white flour
	Grated rind of 1 lemon
2	eggs
1⅓	cups milk
⅓	cup water
⅓	cup yogurt
2	tablespoons mild-flavored oil

For the filling:

2	pounds fresh spinach
1	tablespoon mild-flavored oil
3	medium leeks, white parts only, cleaned and thinly sliced
	Grated rind of 1 lemon
2	teaspoons fresh gingerroot, peeled and grated
	Salt and freshly ground pepper (to taste)
	Yogurt, about 1 teaspoon per crepe

For the sauce:

	Remaining yogurt, approximately 1½ cups
1	teaspoon minced fresh coriander leaves
2	to 3 scallions, finely sliced
	Juice of 1 lemon (or more to taste)
	Freshly ground pepper (to taste)

Sift the flours together into a mixing bowl. Whisk in the lemon rind and make a well in the center of the flour. Beat the eggs, and beat in the milk, water, yogurt, and oil. Add the liquid ingredients to the flour and whisk them together with just a few strokes; don't try to eliminate all the lumps. Cover the bowl and refrigerate.

Wash the spinach and trim off the stems. Place the damp leaves in a large covered saucepan and heat for a few moments to wilt, stirring once or twice (you may need to do this in 2 batches). Drain the spinach in a colander. Heat the oil in a large frying pan and sauté

the leeks for about 5 minutes. Stir in the spinach, lemon rind, and gingerroot, and cook for about 5 minutes, stirring occasionally. Taste the mixture and add salt and pepper as desired.

Spread a damp dish towel on the counter near the stove top. Heat the 8-inch frying pan or crepe pan over medium heat. Take the batter from the refrigerator and stir it once or twice; it should be the consistency of heavy cream. Pour a small amount of batter into the pan, lift the pan and tilt it to coat the bottom evenly with batter. Pour any excess back into the bowl.

Let the crepe cook for 2 to 3 minutes. When the center begins to lift from the pan, use the flexible spatula to loosen the edges and gently fold back the crepe to see if it is beginning to brown. When the crepe is lightly browned you should be able to free it from the pan. Use the spatula to make sure it is completely loose, then invert the pan over the dish towel. If the crepe has not landed flat, cooked side up, gently adjust it. (You may find it easier to lift the crepes out of the pan with your hands.)

As with all pancakes, if your batter is properly mixed, you should not have to grease the cooking pan. If this first crepe was not successful, here are some hints for adjusting the procedure: If the pan is too hot, the crepe will scorch. If the pan is too cool, the crepe will take a long time to cook and will seem to be

Amaranth-dredged Chicken Oriental (right) served on a bed of noodles.

sticking when you check it. If the batter is too thick, the crepes will be too doughy and fat to roll up. To correct this, add a little more milk, but if you add more than ⅓ cup, add 1 teaspoon oil, too. Make another crepe. The procedure is a little tricky, but you will get the hang of it.

If you are making the crepes ahead of time, stack them on a plate or tray with layers of damp paper towel or wax paper between each one, or wrap in plastic wrap and refrigerate. If not, you can fill each crepe as the next one is cooking.

Preheat oven to 375°F.

Lightly oil a large shallow baking dish. While the crepe is still cooked-side-up on the damp towel, spread about a teaspoon of yogurt over the center. Place a small mound of the spinach filling over the yogurt. Fold 2 opposite edges of the crepe over the filling, then fold the 2 remaining edges over the first, making a square or rectangular packet. Gently lift the packet and place it, seam-side down, in the baking dish. Repeat with each crepe, arranging them in one layer in the dish. Use a second dish if the first does not hold all the filled crepes.

Bake the crepes in the preheated oven until they begin to turn golden, about 10 to 12 minutes.

While the crepes are baking, make the yogurt sauce. Mix the remaining yogurt with the coriander, scallions, lemon juice, and pepper. Taste and adjust the seasonings.

Makes 12 to 15 crepes.

Amaranth Chicken Oriental

Another way to take advantage of amaranth's natural stickiness is to use it as a poultry "dredge." The faint vegetable taste of the amaranth is enhanced by the lemon-soy ginger sauce. Serve with a side dish of noodles in soy or sesame sauce.

1	*cup cooked whole amaranth, chilled*
1½	*pounds boneless chicken breasts, cut into bite-size pieces*
	Grated rind and juice of 1 lemon
2	*tablespoons soy sauce*
3	*tablespoons vegetable oil*
1	*carrot, very thinly sliced*
3	*scallions, including green parts, thinly sliced*
1	*1-inch piece fresh gingerroot, peeled and grated or thinly sliced*
1	*clove garlic, minced*

Preheat oven to 350°F.

Put the amaranth on a plate and spread it out a bit. A few pieces at a time, press the chicken into the amaranth, then turn and press again so that all sides are coated. (To prevent the amaranth from sticking to your fingers, dip your hands in cold water.) Transfer the chicken to a plate covered with wax paper (put more paper between subsequent layers if necessary) and set aside.

Whisk together the lemon, soy sauce, and vegetable oil, blending thoroughly. Stir in the vegetables. Place in a flameproof baking dish and heat slowly over low heat. Add the chicken, turning gently to coat with sauce. Cover the pan and bake in preheated oven until the chicken is tender, 12 to 15 minutes.

Makes 4 servings.

Amaranth Drop Cookies

The slightly malty taste of the amaranth itself flavors these simple mounded drop cookies. If you want something fancier, add chocolate chips, nuts, or raisins (or substitute a little grated lemon rind for the vanilla), but spices will obscure the taste of the flour.

½	cup butter
⅓	cup sugar
1	egg, beaten
½	teaspoon vanilla
1	cup amaranth flour
1	teaspoon baking powder

Preheat oven to 350°F.

Cream the butter and the sugar. Add the egg and vanilla and beat until fluffy. Beat in the flour and baking powder. Drop by scant teaspoonfuls 1 inch apart on greased cookie sheets and bake in preheated oven for 10 minutes. Transfer to a wire rack to cool.

Makes two to three dozen 1-inch mounded or 2-inch wafer cookies.

Note: To make a thin wafer cookie, omit ¼ cup flour and ¼ teaspoon baking powder and space the cookies at 2-inch intervals. A pretty golden ring will edge the baked cookies.

Quiche with Amaranth Crust

Cooked whole amaranth grains can be used to make a very easy, slightly crunchy crust that works well for vegetable quiche. A broccoli version, lightly flavored with cumin, is suggested here, but spinach or leeks would work as well. If you like, thyme or oregano and feta cheese can be substituted for the cumin and Gruyère.

For the crust:
2	cups cooked whole amaranth, chilled
	Grated rind of 1 lemon
¼	cup minced fresh parsley
	Salt and freshly ground pepper

For the filling:
1½	cups milk
½	teaspoon crushed cumin seed
2	tablespoons oil
1	small onion, sliced
1	sliced shallot
1½	cups broccoli florets, broken or sliced into small pieces
¾	cup grated Gruyère cheese (optional)
3	eggs, beaten

Preheat oven to 375°F.

To make the crust, combine the amaranth with the lemon rind, parsley, salt and pepper and mix well. Turn the mixture into an oiled 9-inch pie pan. Press the amaranth mixture against the pan, making a thin shell. (To prevent the grain from sticking to your fingers, dip your hands in cold water.) Smooth the top of the shell even with the edge of the pan.

Scald the milk, stir the cumin seed into it, and set aside to cool. Heat the oil over low heat in a large skillet and sauté the onion and shallot until soft, about 10 minutes. Add the broccoli, cover the pan, and continue to cook, stirring frequently, for another 10 minutes, or until it turns bright green.

If using, scatter the grated cheese in the bottom of the amaranth crust. Arrange the vegetables over it. Whisk the eggs and milk mixture together, season with salt and pepper, and pour into the crust (do not overfill). Bake in preheated oven until the custard is firm, about 40 minutes. Serve warm or at room temperature.

Makes one 9-inch quiche.

Barley is one of the oldest cultivated grains. There is some evidence that it was raised in western Asia as long ago as 7,000 B.C.; it was grown in Egypt before 5,000 B.C. It has been used in ancient cultures as an offering to the gods, as a currency, and as a unit of measure. It was treasured for its medicinal as well as nutritive value. In the Middle East, it was used by the ancient Hebrews, Greeks, and Romans to make bread before wheat, with its superior rising qualities, became the common flour. It has been an important staple grain in parts of China and Japan for thousands of years. By the Middle Ages, barley had become a common crop in Europe. It was brought to the New World by Dutch and English colonists, who used it primarily to make beer.

Barley is an adaptable plant and can be grown in many parts of the world. Today it is raised north of the Arctic circle and south nearly to the equator. Much of what is grown in Western cultures is used either as animal feed or malted and fermented for beer. In American cuisine it is most often used pearled—its least nutritious form—as an addition to soup; finding unrefined barley is something of a challenge.

The barley kernel is protected by two layers of inedible husk called spikelets. Under these the endosperm is surrounded by a thin layer called the aleurone; it is in this layer that almost all of barley's fiber and nutrients are stored. Unfortunately, the refining process ap-

A windswept field of barley—one of the oldest known cultivated grains.

plied to barley almost always removes not only the spikelets but the aleurone as well, giving us the familiar white kernels known as pearled barley. However, there is some evidence that barley endosperm houses a substance that inhibits cholesterol production in both humans and animals, meaning that the flesh (and eggs) of barley-fed animals is lower in cholesterol than usual for its type. High cholesterol–related heart disease is rare in areas of the world where barley is a dietary staple.

Pearling is the process by which barley is refined. The whole grains are placed in a perforated cylinder in which revolving abrasive disks grind off the hulls, aleurone, and germ. The kernels turn constantly so that the pearling is even. They are processed for a few minutes, placed on a screen where the chaff is sifted off, and then returned to the cylinders for additional pearling. The more barley is pearled, the whiter it becomes. If you are interested in using barley in its most nutritious form, try to purchase the brownest kernels (the least processed) you can find.

Barley has a faint, slightly sweet but bland taste. You can complement it with either rich creamy sauces or hearty savory ones. It is traditionally served with beef or lamb, meaty vegetables such as mushrooms, or fruit.

Hulled Barley

Pearled Barley

Barley Flour

Hulled (and Hull-less) Groats

Hulled barley is the whole barley kernel with only the spikelet removed. It can be sprouted or cooked as a whole-grain side dish and served like rice. In this form barley is an excellent source of dietary fiber—perhaps better than an equivalent amount of whole wheat—and provides protein and B vitamins. Barley is also at its most flavorful with the aleurone layer intact. Hull-less barley is a particular strain that grows, of course, without a hull.

Pearled Barley

Pearled barley has been through six pearlings. Most of the nutrients and fiber are removed, and it has only a mild flavor. It can be served as a side dish (some people add plenty of cream) or mixed into casseroles, but its most traditional use is in vegetable and beef soups. If you plan to serve it as a simple side dish, you might cook it in stock to give its mild flavor a bit of a boost. Pearled barley quadruples in volume when it is

cooked, so be sparing when adding to soups—it can turn a tasty broth into a glutinous mush.

Pot Barley

Pot barley, sometimes called Scotch barley, has been through three pearlings. It retains some of the aleurone layer and thus some of the nutrients. It is not easy to find, but you may be able to ask your health-food store to order it for you. It can be prepared as a side dish or added to soups in the same way you would use pearled barley, but may require a somewhat longer cooking time.

Cracked

Cracked barley, or barley grits, is made from toasted whole hulled barley kernels that have been broken into many pieces. They are usually prepared as a breakfast cereal and can be cooked in either water or milk in about fifteen minutes. Like oatmeal, barley porridge can be fried to make griddle cakes.

Flour

Barley flour is most often made from pearled barley, although sometimes it is made from the siftings culled from the pearling process and sometimes from whole hulled barley. You can find it in health-food stores. It is one of the oldest flours known to man, and was used to bake bread before wheat flour. It has very little gluten, so it must be mixed with other flours to make a yeast-raised bread, although some people believe that the maltose (natural sugar) content helps the yeast to grow. It can be substituted for wheat flour in quick breads and used to thicken soups or gravies, a fact that should be remembered by those with a wheat allergy.

Malted

Malted barley is made from whole barley that has been sprouted and toasted. It is used to brew beer or to add a characteristic flavor to milk shakes or other sweets. You can make malt by spreading barley sprouts (see page 101) on a cookie sheet and toasting them in a 250°F oven for about 20 minutes, then grinding them in a food grinder. If necessary, sift out any remaining bits of hull.

BARLEY RECIPES

Basic Steamed Barley Groats

Hulled and hull-less barley groats double in volume when steamed; pearled barley quadruples in volume.

The exact proportion of water to grain and the length of the cooking time will vary somewhat in each individual kitchen—the size and weight of the pan, the intensity of the flame, and the desired degree of softness all influence the results. The directions that follow are for grains that are cooked but discrete; if you wish to make a creamy porridge, increase both the amount of water and the cooking time.

Place 1 part hulled barley groats and 2 parts water, or 1 part pearled barley and 3 parts water, in a saucepan. Bring to a boil, cover, reduce the heat, and simmer for 30 minutes.

Fluff the cooked barley with a fork and serve with butter, yogurt, or soy sauce, or use in recipes calling for cooked whole barley. You can use this basic recipe as a guideline when adding barley to soup.

Barley Flour Pecan Scones (above right) make a tasty breakfast or teatime treat.

Barley Flour Pecan Scones

These are good scones; they are not too sweet and can be prepared quickly.

1	cup barley flour
1	cup all-purpose flour
2	tablespoons sugar, plus additional for glaze
1½	teaspoons baking powder
½	teaspoon baking soda
	Pinch of salt
4	tablespoons butter, chilled
2	eggs, beaten (reserve a little for glaze)
½	cup yogurt, mixed with 1 tablespoon water
½	cup broken pecan meats, plus 8 pecan halves

Preheat oven to 400°F.

Mix all of the dry ingredients except the pecans together in a bowl. Cut in the butter with a pastry blender until pea-size. Add the eggs and yogurt. Using a fork, mix together with a few quick strokes. Turn the dough onto a lightly floured board, flatten, sprinkle with the broken pecan meats, and knead together for a few moments (if the dough is too sticky to handle, add a little more all-purpose flour). Roll the dough into a round about ½ inch thick. Cut into 8 pie-shape wedges. Place the wedges about ½ inch apart on a buttered cookie sheet. Brush the tops with egg, press a pecan half onto each section, brush a little egg onto the pecan halves, and sprinkle the scones with a bit of sugar. Bake in preheated oven for 15 minutes.

Makes 8 scones.

Barley Pilaf with Mushrooms and Dill

Wild mushrooms give this a special flavor. If serving with a meat dish, use an appropriately flavored broth. Garnish with sour cream and a bit more dill, if you like.

1   ounce dried mushrooms, such as shiitake or porcini
1   cup hot water
2   tablespoons butter, more if needed
10 ounces fresh white or cremini mushrooms, cleaned and sliced
1   parsnip or carrot, chopped
3   shallots, peeled and chopped
1   onion, chopped
1½ cups hulled or ¾ cup pearled barley
2   cups water or broth, more if needed
2   tablespoons chopped fresh dill
    Salt and freshly ground pepper (to taste)

Soak the dried mushrooms in the hot water for 1 hour. Drain through a coffee filter and reserve the liquid. Rinse the mushrooms in cold water and pick out any dirt. Dry and chop the mushrooms.

Melt the butter in a flameproof casserole. Add the chopped and fresh mushrooms and the parsnip or carrot, shallots, and onion. Sauté over medium heat, stirring frequently, until just brown, about 10 minutes. Add the barley and stir to coat. Add the reserved liquid from the dried mushrooms and the water or broth. Bring to a boil, cover, reduce the heat, and simmer until the barley is not quite tender, about 20 minutes. Stir in the dill and salt and pepper, adding more liquid if necessary, and continue to simmer until the barley is done, about 10 minutes more.

Makes 6 servings.

Barley Flour Rye Bread

Here is a hearty, flavorful bread. It has no wheat, so the recipe makes a low loaf, but it is not heavy. Serve it with vegetable soup and cheese, or toast it for breakfast.

1   package yeast (cake or fresh)
2   cups warm water
2   tablespoons molasses or honey
2   tablespoons oil
1   teaspoon salt
1   tablespoon caraway seeds
3   cups barley flour
2   cups rye flour

Dissolve the yeast in the warm water in a large mixing bowl. Gently stir in the molasses or honey. Let the mixture rest for about 10 minutes until the yeast begins to bubble. Stir in the oil, salt, and caraway seeds. One cup at a time, stir in most of the flours. Turn the dough onto a floured pastry board and knead until smooth and elastic, working in more flour as necessary. Shape the dough into a ball.

Oil a large bowl; place the dough in the bowl, turning once to oil the top. Cover with a damp cloth and put in a warm place. Allow to rise until doubled in size, 1 to 1½ hours.

Preheat oven to 375°F.

Punch the dough down and knead it briefly on the floured board. Divide into 2 pieces and let rest while you oil 2 loaf pans. Shape the dough into loaves and place in the pans. Rub a little oil on your hands and pat the tops of the loaves. Bake in preheated oven for 50 minutes. Remove from the pans to cool.

Makes 2 loaves.

Scotch Broth

A hearty soup of lamb, vegetables, and barley.

1   tablespoon vegetable oil
3   pounds lamb, with bones
3   quarts water
1   whole onion
1   clove garlic
1   whole carrot
1   cup hulled or ½ cup pearled barley
1   onion, peeled and diced
1   carrot, sliced or diced
1   small turnip, peeled and diced
2   stalks celery, sliced
1   3- to 4-inch sprig of fresh rosemary
    Salt and freshly ground pepper (to taste)
¼   cup chopped fresh parsley

Heat the oil in a large stockpot and brown the meat (do this in batches, if necessary). Add the water and onion, garlic clove, and carrot. Bring to a boil, cover, reduce heat, and simmer for 1½ hours. Remove the vegetables and discard. If necessary, remove the meat and cut into small pieces or remove from the bone (if desired), then return to the pot. Add the barley and simmer for 15 minutes. Add the cut-up vegetables and the rosemary. Simmer until the barley is tender, another 15 to 20 minutes.

Season with salt and pepper and garnish with fresh parsley.

Makes ten to twelve 1-cup servings.

Choose Barley Pilaf with Mushrooms and Dill (left) to complement an otherwise simple meal.

Buckwheat is neither a member of the wheat family nor a true grain. *Boekweit* is a Dutch word meaning "beech wheat"; buckwheat seeds are similar in shape to beechnuts and share many of the same nutritional values as wheat. Buckwheat is a branching plant with heart-shaped leaves and clusters of extremely fragrant flowers, and is not a grass but a relative of rhubarb and dock. However, in our cuisine, it finds a logical home among the cereal grains. In addition, buckwheat flowers give a strong flavor to honey; they rely upon bees for pollination and stay in bloom for about thirty days.

Buckwheat is probably a native of central and western China, where it is used in bread. From the Orient, it was carried to Eastern Europe by migrating tribes; there it is most often used as porridge or pilaf. Buckwheat was brought to the New World by Dutch and English settlers, who planted it in the Hudson Valley. Buckwheat tolerates poor growing conditions and is naturally pest-resistant. At one time it was a major crop in the United States, but this is no longer so. Most of the buckwheat raised today is grown in the Soviet Union.

Buckwheat has a strong taste, and while cooking, the whole grain forms give off a particular aroma. Buckwheat is extremely nutritious, as it's high in protein, has some of the B vitamins and several important minerals, and contains no fat. When buckwheat is processed, only the inedible outer hull is removed;

the nutrient-rich, fibrous layer is always left on the kernels, which are called groats. This layer is not removed when the groats are further processed. Most people are familiar with buckwheat pancakes; if you have never tried the groats, you will find them tasty, naturally quick-cooking, and easy to prepare. They are readily available in their roasted form (kasha) in most grocery stores as well as at many markets catering to Jewish and Eastern European customers.

Buckwheat in flower.

Buckwheat is the most intensely flavored of the grains. Complement it with mild or savory but not spicy foods. Serve it with eggs, poultry, game, or hearty fish such as carp or cod. Butter, onions, mushrooms, and ground pepper are traditional seasonings. Buckwheat is also very good garnished with natural sweets—honey or maple syrup—and jam or fresh fruits such as apples. Baked goods made with buckwheat flour are delicious at breakfast or teatime.

© Grant Heilman

WHAT TO LOOK FOR IN THE MARKET

Buckwheat Groats

Kasha

Buckwheat Flour

Groats

Buckwheat groats are three-sided; they are about half the size of long-grain rice and are quite attractive, especially when roasted. Hulled, unroasted groats are most often used to make porridge. They can also be sprouted (see page 101); the sprouts are a tasty addition to salad.

Grits

Unroasted buckwheat groats are sometimes cracked into smaller pieces called grits. They can be used to make porridge. Buckwheat grits are sometimes used as a meat extender, particularly in some kinds of sausage.

Kasha

Kasha is the name given to roasted hulled buckwheat groats. Roasting turns the groats a rich golden color and enhances their flavor. Kasha is available in several forms—whole, or cracked into coarse, medium, or fine grits. Kasha can be added to soups, prepared as a plain side dish or as pilaf, and it is very good as a stuffing for poultry or strong-flavored fish. The medium and fine grades are best prepared as porridge.

Flour

Buckwheat flour is ground from un-roasted groats. It varies from light to dark gray in tone, the flecks of deeper color indicating that part of the hull remains. Buckwheat flour has no gluten, so it must be mixed with gluten-rich flour when making yeast-raised bread. However, it is traditionally used as the sole flour in Russian *blini* (yeast-raised pancakes) and in the dessert crepes typical of the northwest area of France. Buckwheat flour adds a characteristic flavor to baked goods (the darker the color, the stronger the flavor); when making biscuits or pancakes it can be substituted easily for part of the wheat flour. The amount really depends upon your taste preference.

BUCKWHEAT RECIPES

Basic Steamed Buckwheat Groats

Whole buckwheat groats double in volume when they are steamed. (See below for basic directions for kasha.)

The exact proportion of water to grain and the length of the cooking time will vary somewhat in each individual kitchen; the size and weight of the pan, the intensity of the flame, and the desired degree of softness all influence the results. The directions that follow are for grains that are cooked but discrete; if you wish to make a creamy porridge, increase both the amount of water and the cooking time.

Place 1 part whole buckwheat groats and 1½ parts water in a saucepan. Bring to a boil, cover, reduce the heat, and simmer for 15 minutes.

Fluff the cooked buckwheat with a fork and serve with butter, yogurt, or soy sauce, or use in recipes calling for cooked whole buckwheat groats. You can use this basic recipe as a guide when adding buckwheat to soup.

How to Cook Kasha

Kasha also doubles in volume when cooked.

Kasha can be cooked following the directions for cooking whole buckwheat groats (allow 1½ parts liquid to 1 part grain), but bear in mind that the cooking time will vary depending upon the degree of coarseness of the grind. In general, whole kasha will cook in about 20 minutes and each finer grind will cook more quickly.

The traditional way to prepare kasha is to mix a beaten egg with the raw grits and cook them in a dry skillet, stirring constantly until they are dry and separate. Then add boiling liquid, cover, reduce the heat, and simmer until tender. Kasha is often cooked in broth if it is to be used as pilaf. Sometimes kasha, with or without the egg, is added to onions that have been sautéed in butter. Kasha is delicious with pepper and butter, sour cream, or yogurt. It is also very good with poached eggs.

Kasha Varnishkas

The combination of kasha and egg noodles is traditional in Jewish cuisine. This is a very easy dish to prepare, and if you stock both kasha and noodles in your kitchen, you can whip it up when your cupboard seems bare.

3	*quarts water*
½	*pound bow-tie egg noodles*
1	*tablespoon butter or oil*
1	*onion, finely sliced*
1	*egg*
1	*cup kasha, whole or coarse grade*
2	*cups boiling water or broth* *Salt and freshly ground pepper (to taste)*

Bring the 3 quarts of water to a boil. Cook the egg noodles in the water until done. Drain and keep warm.

Meanwhile, melt the butter or oil in a skillet or heavy saucepan over low heat. Sauté the onion until transparent, about 7 minutes. Beat the egg in a small mixing bowl and stir in the kasha, coating all the grains. Add the kasha to the sautéed onion and stir until the egg is dry. Add the boiling water or broth, cover, reduce the heat, and simmer until done. Season with salt and pepper. Stir in the hot noodles and mix well.

Makes 4 to 6 servings.

Kasha and egg noodles are the primary ingredients of Kasha Varnishkas (right). Of course, the shape of the noodles has no effect on the taste, so choose whatever is available.

Yeast-Raised Buckwheat Pancakes

These delicious, light pancakes are wonderful served with maple syrup. They are also very good as a main course when topped with yogurt and steamed spinach, or as dessert with fresh fruit.

The batter should be mixed the night before you plan to cook it. If desired, ½ cup of white flour may be substituted for a like amount of buckwheat flour. Leftover batter can be refrigerated; allow it to reach room temperature before cooking.

The cakes will scorch if the griddle is too hot, so cook a test cake and adjust the temperature if necessary.

2   *cups milk*
1   *tablespoon molasses*
¼   *package yeast (cake or fresh)*
½   *teaspoon salt*
2   *tablespoons oil*
1¾ *cups buckwheat flour*
1   *egg or 2 egg whites or ¼ teaspoon baking soda dissolved in ¼ cup lukewarm water*

Scald the milk. Stir in the molasses and let the mixture cool to lukewarm. Place the yeast in a large mixing bowl and pour the milk over it, stirring gently to dissolve the yeast. Stir in the salt, oil, and about ¼ cup of the flour. Let the mixture rest for about 10 minutes, until the yeast begins to bubble. Stir in the rest of the flour. Cover the bowl with a damp cloth and let rise overnight (10 to 12 hours).

Preheat a griddle or heavy frying pan over low heat. If using, beat the egg or egg whites. Gently fold the egg or soda-water mixture into the batter. Drop the batter off a large serving spoon onto the griddle. Cook the pancakes until bubbles rise to the surface and just begin to break, then flip and cook a few minutes longer. Place on a plate in a warm oven until ready to serve.

Makes about sixteen 5-inch pancakes.

Quick Buckwheat Breakfast "Scramble"

Here it is, as good as pancakes, eggless and practically fat-free. Serve with maple syrup.

1½ *cups cooked buckwheat groats (or kasha)*
1   *apple, cored and cut into chunks*
        Small amount of butter (or to taste)

Heat a well-seasoned skillet over a medium flame. Add the buckwheat groats and the apple and stir constantly until heated through and the apple begins to soften. If the mixture sticks to the skillet, add a little butter (or add a lot if you are feeling indulgent). Serve immediately, topped with maple syrup.

Serves 2.

Buckwheat flour has a distinctive taste that is enticingly complemented by fresh fruit and other sweet condiments. It is traditionally used to make Yeast-Raised Pancakes (left).

Buckwheat Flour Skillet Bread

If you visualize gingerbread and taste kasha, you will have an accurate impression of this quick bread. It is not sweet and, like buckwheat pancakes, it is delicious topped with jam. For some reason the flavor seems to improve after a day or two, so don't feel it is wasted if you can't eat it all fresh from the oven. Bake this in a 9-inch skillet and cut in wedges to serve.

1½ cups buckwheat flour
¾ cup all-purpose flour
½ teaspoon salt
½ teaspoon baking soda
4 tablespoons butter, melted
2 tablespoons molasses
1 cup milk
½ cup yogurt
1 egg

Preheat oven to 375°F.

Mix the dry ingredients together in a mixing bowl and make a well in the center. Brush the inside of a 9-inch skillet with a light coat of the melted butter, then dissolve the molasses in the remaining butter. Combine the milk, yogurt, and egg and beat together. Add the butter and molasses and the milk mixtures to the dry ingredients and stir until blended. The batter will be quite stiff. Spoon the dough into the skillet and bake in preheated oven for about 40 minutes. Be careful not to overbake this bread; remove it from the oven when a tester comes out clean.

Makes one 9-inch-round bread.

Kasha Pilaf with Broccoli and Mushrooms

This is a good choice for a cold night. Be sure not to overcook the broccoli or it will lose its complementary color and crunch. If you like, crumble some feta cheese over the casserole before you put it in the oven.

1 ounce dried mushrooms, such as shiitake or porcini
1½ cups hot water
2 tablespoons butter (or more if needed)
3 shallots, peeled and chopped
1 onion, chopped
1 egg
1 cup kasha, whole or coarse grade
10 ounces fresh white or cremini mushrooms, cleaned and sliced
½ cup water or broth
½ cup yogurt or sour cream
2 cups broccoli florets
   Salt and freshly ground pepper (to taste)

Soak the dried mushrooms in the hot water for 1 hour. Drain through a coffee filter and reserve the liquid in a small saucepan. Rinse the mushrooms in cold water and pick out any dirt. Dry and chop the mushrooms.

Preheat oven to 375°F.

Bring the reserved soaking liquid to a boil and keep it simmering. Melt 1

tablespoon of butter in a flameproof casserole. Add the shallots and onion and sauté over medium heat, stirring frequently, until they begin to brown, about 10 minutes. Beat the egg in a small mixing bowl and stir the kasha into it, coating all the grains. Add the kasha to the sautéed onion and stir until the egg is dry. Add the boiling reserved liquid, cover, reduce the heat, and simmer until the kasha is not quite tender, about 10 to 15 minutes (if the kasha absorbs all the liquid before the next step is complete, remove it from the heat for a moment).

Meanwhile, heat the remaining butter in a skillet over medium heat. Sauté the soaked and fresh mushrooms in it until richly colored, about 15 minutes. Add the mushrooms to the kasha. Mix the water or broth with the yogurt or sour cream and stir into the kasha. Place the casserole, uncovered, in preheated oven and continue to cook until the kasha is done and begins to brown, about 15 minutes more. (If you continue to simmer it on top of the stove, the yogurt could curdle.) While the kasha bakes, steam the broccoli until it is bright green. Stir the broccoli into the kasha and season with salt and pepper.

Makes 4 to 6 servings.

The tart accent of the yogurt in Kasha Pilaf with Broccoli and Mushrooms (right) complements Kabobs perfectly.

CORN

© Christopher C. Bain

Corn has been domesticated and hybridized for so many thousands of years that no one knows exactly what the original wild grain was like. The ancestor of the corn we know today grew wild in Central and South America. It was farmed by the Aztecs and Mayans and gradually carried to North America. Over the centuries the Indians of the Americas transformed the wild grain, adapting it so that it would grow almost anywhere in the hemisphere. In the process, the plant lost its ability to reproduce in the wild; the husk over each ear so completely protects the kernels (seeds) that they are not able to disperse of their own accord, but must be deliberately sown. Incidentally, the silk that tops each ear of corn contains the pollen; when it is pollinated, each strand of silk initiates the growth of an individual kernel on the cob.

Christopher Columbus carried the corn he found in the New World back to Spain, and within a few decades it was being cultivated around the world. Interestingly, through most of its history, corn was usually dried and ground before it was eaten. The vegetable sweet corn, which is eaten fresh with such relish while it is in season, was not developed until the seventeenth century.

Today corn is an incredibly important crop worldwide (wheat is the only crop that covers more acreage), and is used primarily to feed livestock. A small percentage of the crop is ground into meal or flour, or used to make cornstarch,

corn syrup, or alcoholic beverages. Most humans derive very little food value from corn, unless they eat a lot of popcorn!

Corn kernels are larger than the whole seeds of any other grains. The outer skin (hull) does not have much nutritional value; it houses two starchy layers and the protein-rich germ. Corn is a fairly good source of B vitamins, vitamins C and A (the yellower the corn, the more vitamin A), potassium, and fiber. Unfortunately, the oils in the germ cause it to spoil rather quickly once the kernels have been cracked or ground. Most of the cornmeal available today has had the germ removed in order to prevent this, so it is missing its natural protein content. Like white wheat flour,

cornmeal and flour without the germ are often sold enriched. If you buy uncooked, refined corn products (grits, meal, or flour) that still contain the germ, be sure to refrigerate them. And if you are eating fresh corn, or removing it from the cob to cook or freeze, cut close to the cob so that you get the germ with the juicy part of the kernels.

The taste of corn is strong enough to be distinctive but not so intense that it fights with other flavors, so think of it as a versatile staple grain. Complement it with sweet, savory, or spicy foods as you wish. A basic corn recipe could be seasoned successfully with honey, herbs, chili peppers, fruit, or cheese, depending upon where you wish to place it in your menu.

VARIETIES

There are several varieties of cultivated corn. They are distinguished by the amount and arrangement of hard starch in the kernel; the character of this starch defines the way each type is used. Most types can be either yellow or white. The *blue* corn grown in the southwestern United States is usually ground into meal or flour. Its steel color is very much in vogue in the cuisine of that region; some people feel its flavor is more intense than that of other corns.

Dent corn is grown primarily for animal feed, but it is also the corn from which most cornmeal and flour are ground. The starch in the kernels is arranged so that the hard part lies along the sides and the soft part is in the center and top. An indentation forms at the top of each kernel as it dries, giving this variety its name.

Flint corn is grown for animal feed; the soft starch in its kernels is completely surrounded by the hard starch. There is some thought that it is quite like the corn that was grown by the North American Indians when the colonists first came to this continent.

Flour corn kernels have a high proportion of soft starch, so they are easily ground into meal or flour. Flour corn is raised by American Indians and is not widely available.

Pod corn is unlike the corn we are accustomed to seeing, because each kernel has its own husk. It is of virtually no interest as a food, but its unusual structure may resemble the way this ancient grain first grew in the wild.

Popcorn kernels are smaller than those of dent corn, and they grow on smaller ears. They have a high hard-starch content that "explodes" through the hull when heated. They are a reasonably good-for-you snack food (particularly when compared to oil-heavy chips) as long as you don't drown them in butter or cheese.

Sweet corn kernels contain a high percentage of sugar. They shrivel when dried and are of little use for grinding, but sweet corn is certainly well-loved as a fresh summer vegetable.

WHAT TO LOOK FOR IN THE MARKET

Kernels

Whole dried corn kernels contain all the nutrients of corn. Unlike the other grains, individual corn kernels do not have an inedible protective hull that must be removed before they can be eaten—the husk that covers the ear serves that purpose. The kernels can be soaked and reconstituted and added to soups or casseroles. If you have an appropriate grinder, you can make your own wholesome processed corn in batches small enough to use before they spoil. However, dried whole-kernel corn is not particularly easy to find; if you are planning to reconstitute it, you will probably find it easier to use frozen kernels. Likewise, you may find wholesome cornmeal at the health-food store more easily than whole kernels. Popcorn is a particular variety of corn; the basic recipe is discussed on page 32.

Hominy

Hominy is whole corn with the hull removed. The American Indians made it by boiling kernels in wood lye (ashes and water) until the hull was soft enough to be rubbed off. Today it is made by soaking and then boiling the kernels in water and baking soda. Hominy is often dried after it is processed; it is also available canned. Sometimes it is cracked into grits.

Corn Grits

Grits

Corn grits are whole dried kernels that have been cracked into coarse, small pieces. They can be cooked as porridge and make excellent polenta (Italian-style mush that definitely belongs in a cuisine that is more sophisticated than the name "grits" implies). You can also soak them and add them to pancakes, muffins, or bread where they lend a pleasant chewiness.

Cornmeal

Corn Flour

Basic Popcorn

When popped, popcorn increases to about eight times its original volume. Use an electric air popper to pop popcorn without oil (follow the manufacturer's directions). Otherwise use a heavy saucepan or skillet with a cover. Heat 1 tablespoon of vegetable oil, add ½ cup popcorn, and cover and cook, keeping the pan in constant motion, for about 2 minutes. (Do not remove the lid while the pan is on the heat or you may be showered with popping corn.) Discard any unopened kernels.

Season popcorn when it is hot. Sprinkle it with grated Parmesan cheese or a blend of herbs and spices. If you are feeling indulgent, toss it with melted butter and salt.

Meal

Cornmeal is coarsely ground dried kernels. Sometimes it is available stoneground. The germ may or may not have been removed, so read the label. It is the usual ingredient of pancakes, muffins, and quick breads; it is sometimes added to yeast bread, particularly anadama or pumpernickel. Cornmeal can be used to make polenta or to dredge meat, fish, or poultry. If used to dust bread pans before the dough is put in to rise, it will add a little crunch to the crust.

Flour

Corn flour is finely ground dried kernels. It is sometimes available stoneground. It lacks gluten, so must be combined with gluten-rich flours when making yeast-raised bread. Tortillas and corn chips are made from corn flour.

Blue Cornmeal

Polenta

In many parts of Europe cornmeal mush, served simply or with embellishment, holds an important position on the menu. In northern Italy it is called polenta, in the Soviet Union, *mamaliga*, in France, *millas*. The basic ingredients are cornmeal and water, with salt and butter to bring out the flavor. It can be served soft, just as it begins to set, or poured into a pan and allowed to become firm, then sliced and fried or even used to make a lasagna-type dish called polenta pasticciata. Soft polenta is often served with Gorgonzola or Parmesan cheese, cream, or sautéed mushrooms. Eastern Europeans top it with feta cheese and bake it until brown and bubbly. Specialty-food shops carry all sorts of seasoned polenta mixes, but there is no trick to making your own—just add small amounts of one or more herbs (fresh if possible) to taste.

Serve polenta with a hearty soup or a big salad, or as a first course. If you rethink the seasonings, it is terrific for breakfast. The following is a basic recipe, with suggestions for seasonings. By the way, you can prepare corn grits in exactly the same way; they will take longer to absorb the water, but make a nicely textured mixture.

For soft polenta:

2 cups water
½ teaspoon salt (or to taste)
½ cup cornmeal
2 tablespoons butter
  Freshly ground pepper (to taste)

Bring the water and salt to a boil in a heavy saucepan. Very slowly, stirring constantly, add the cornmeal. Reduce the heat so the mixture simmers, and stir constantly until all the water has been absorbed and the polenta is tender, about 15 minutes. Stir in the butter and pepper. Spoon into bowls or plates and garnish as desired.

Makes four ½-cup servings.

For firm polenta:

Prepare the polenta in exactly the same way, but make at least twice the recipe so that you will have enough to fill a loaf pan. When the polenta is ready, turn into a pan lined with greased wax paper, cool to room temperature, and refrigerate for several hours or overnight to set. When firm, remove from the pan, peel off the paper, and slice and prepare as desired.

Makes eight ½-cup servings.

Variations:

Add ¼ cup crumbled, room temperature Gorgonzola cheese to the basic recipe when stirring in the butter.

Top the basic recipe with grated fresh Parmesan cheese and minced fresh parsley.

Stir fresh herbs into the polenta while it is cooking. Some that work well with the corn flavor are thyme, oregano, rosemary, tarragon, and fennel (dill tastes good as well, although it is not typical of this cuisine).

Turn the polenta into a greased baking dish and top with crumbled or grated cheese of your choice (mixed with herbs or minced garlic if desired) and bake at 375°F until brown, about 12 minutes.

Top basic polenta with your favorite meat or vegetable spaghetti sauce.

Dredge slices of firm polenta in cornmeal and pan-fry in butter. Serve with spaghetti sauce, sautéed mushrooms, and onions or grated cheese.

Dredge slices of firm polenta in cornmeal, pan-fry in butter, and serve with maple syrup or fresh fruit for a delicious egg- and milk-free alternative to pancakes. (If you like, you can add blueberries or other fruit to the basic polenta while it is cooking; if you are watching your cholesterol, substitute vegetable oil for butter.)

Try this variation when you are feeling indulgent: make a sandwich with two slices of firm polenta and ham and cheese (use prosciutto and provolone if you like), dip in egg and dredge in cornmeal, then pan-fry until heated through.

Plain, unbuttered popcorn (left) is a truly good-for-you snack food.

Polenta Pasticciata

Olive oil and butter, as needed for frying

8 to **10** *½-inch-thick slices of Firm Polenta (page 33), cut to fit in 2 layers in a 7- by 10-inch baking dish*

2 *cups Classic Tomato or Classic Meat sauce (page 113)*

¼ *cup ricotta cheese*

½ *cup freshly grated Parmesan cheese*

Preheat oven to 450°F.

Heat 1 tablespoon each of oil and butter in a heavy skillet over medium-low heat. Put in as many slices of polenta as will fit comfortably and sauté for about 7 minutes on each side. Transfer the slices to a plate and repeat, adding more oil and butter as necessary, with the remaining slices.

Arrange a layer of polenta slices in the bottom of the baking dish. Pour half the tomato sauce over the slices. Scatter half the ricotta over the sauce, and top with half the Parmesan. Repeat the process to make another layer.

Place the dish in the preheated oven and bake until the cheese is bubbling and golden, 15 to 20 minutes. Remove from the oven and let stand for a few minutes before serving.

Makes 6 servings.

Polenta Pasticciata (left) is similar to lasagna but made with layers of polenta (cornmeal mush) instead of pasta. Use the recipe given here as a beginning and elaborate as inspiration strikes.

Corn Bread and Chestnut Turkey Stuffing

This is a moist, flavorful cornucopia of a dressing. If you are planning it for an early meal, like the traditional American Thanksgiving, make the corn bread and peel the chestnuts the night before so that you will be able to assemble it in good time for your roasting schedule. If there is never enough leftover stuffing for your family, double the recipe (you'll need 2 mixing bowls) and bake a batch (basted with turkey drippings) in a covered casserole.

12 to **18** *chestnuts*

1 *recipe Basic Savory Corn Bread (page 36), seasoned with rosemary and thyme*

1 *tart apple, cored and cut in chunks*

1 *onion, peeled and coarsely chopped*

1 *large stalk celery, coarsely chopped*

1 *teaspoon fresh rosemary and thyme, minced*

   Salt and freshly ground pepper (to taste)

1 *egg beaten with 2 tablespoons water, or ¼ cup stock*

To peel the chestnuts easily, place them in a small saucepan and cover with water. Bring to a boil, then remove the pan from the heat. Using a slotted spoon, remove the nuts one at a time and, with a paring knife, peel off both the shell and the inner skin. Discard any flesh that is moldy. Cut the chestnuts into small pieces and put in a large mixing bowl.

Cut or break the corn bread into 1 to 1½-inch chunks and add to the bowl. Add the apple, onion, celery, and seasonings. Mix the ingredients well. Add the beaten egg or the stock and mix again. Fill the turkey cavity loosely.

Makes 2 quarts stuffing, enough for a 14- to 16-pound turkey.

Note: This recipe is really only the beginning; you can vary or add to the ingredients as you wish. Leeks and mushrooms are good additions, for instance.

Basic Corn Muffins

1¼ cups cornmeal
¾   cup all-purpose flour
1½ teaspoons baking powder
½   teaspoon baking soda
½   teaspoon salt (optional)
1   cup milk
2   eggs, beaten
¼   cup butter, melted with 2 tablespoons
    honey

Preheat oven to 400°F.

Mix all the dry ingredients together in a bowl and make a well in the center. Add the milk, eggs, butter, and honey and stir together quickly. Spoon into greased or paper-lined muffin tins, filling them about two-thirds full. Bake in preheated oven about 20 minutes, or until golden and firm and a tester inserted in one comes out clean. Remove from the tin at once.

Makes 12 muffins.

Variations:

Add ½ cup raisins, chopped nuts, or chopped fresh fruit to the batter before baking.

Add ¼ teaspoon cinnamon or nutmeg to the dry ingredients.

Cream 1 tablespoon butter with 1 tablespoon brown sugar, sprinkle on top of the muffins, and top with a walnut or pecan half before baking.

Basic Savory Cornbread (right) is not sweet and can be a quick and easy accompaniment to a homemade meal— make it plain or add seasonings that enhance your main dish.

Indian Pudding

A classic New England dessert, Indian pudding is really sweetened cornmeal mush made with milk instead of water. For best results, make it in a double boiler.

4   cups milk
⅔   cup cornmeal
¾   cup molasses
¼   cup butter, cut in small pieces
½   teaspoon salt
½   teaspoon nutmeg
½   teaspoon cinnamon
½   teaspoon ginger
½   cup raisins (optional)

Preheat oven to 325°F.

In the top of a double boiler, scald 3 cups of the milk directly over the heat. Place over boiling water and very slowly add the cornmeal, stirring constantly. Cook uncovered for about 15 minutes. Stir in the molasses and cook another 5 minutes or until thickened. Add the butter, stirring until it melts. Stir in the salt, spices, and raisins and turn the mixture into a buttered baking dish. Smooth with a spoon or spatula, then pour the remaining cup of milk over the batter. Bake in preheated oven for about 2 hours; the pudding will be soft. Serve warm.

Makes 6 servings.

Basic Savory Corn Bread

Use this recipe if you plan to serve corn bread at lunch or dinner or want to use it as the base for poultry stuffing. Use a preheated heavy baking dish so that the edges of the bread are crisped nicely.

1½ cups cornmeal
½   cup all-purpose flour
1½ teaspoons baking powder
½   teaspoon baking soda
½   teaspoon salt (optional)
1   cup buttermilk
2   eggs, beaten
¼   cup oil or melted butter

Preheat the oven to 425°F.

Have all of the ingredients out and measured. Oil a 9- by 7-inch glass baking pan (or a 9-inch cast-iron skillet) and put it in the oven to heat while you mix the bread. Mix all the dry ingredients together in a bowl and make a well in the center. Add the buttermilk, eggs, and oil or butter and stir together quickly. Pour into the heated baking dish and bake in preheated oven until the bread pulls away from the sides of the pan and begins to crisp, about 25 to 30 minutes.

Makes one 9- by 7-inch bread.

Variations:

Add 1 teaspoon (or to taste) fresh savory herbs such as dill, tarragon, sage, thyme, or rosemary to the batter.

Add ¼ to ½ cup chopped red or green bell pepper, chopped onion, or crumbled bacon to the batter. Add chopped hot chilies and shredded jack cheese if you are planning a Mexican meal.

Millet is a small, round buff-colored grain important to the cuisines of North Africa and India. Because it tolerates poor growing conditions, it is a staple grain in many other parts of the world. Although it was a common dietary crop in medieval Europe, millet is used primarily as bird and poultry food in contemporary Western cultures. However, millet shares the nutritional value of other grains, cooks quickly, and has a pleasant flavor not unlike sweet corn, so it is worthy of inclusion in our cuisine. It can take a place on the menu like that often filled by rice. It is the grain traditionally used for couscous (the packaged couscous commonly available is usually a wheat-based form of pasta) and people with wheat allergies should be pleased to incorporate it into their diets. Look for it in the specialty-food section of your grocery, or at a health-food store.

Like corn, the taste of millet is strong enough to be distinctive but not so intense that it fights with other flavors. In addition, the whole groats are readily available and can be served like rice, so it is a truly versatile grain. Complement it with sweet, savory, or spicy foods as you wish. It has a pretty pale-yellow color when cooked, so think of its visual as well as taste attributes when planning a meal.

WHAT TO LOOK FOR IN THE MARKET

Millet Groats

Millet Couscous

Whole Millet Groats

Unlike birdseed, the whole millet sold for people has been hulled, and is sometimes called pearl millet. Like rice, it is usually cooked separately and added to other ingredients to make casseroles, pilafs, salads, and the like. It can be used as a meat extender, added to soups, and is tasty in egg-and-milk–based dishes like puddings and soufflés. Millet groats can be sprouted and then added to salads.

Cracked (Couscous)

Millet couscous has been steamed and cracked, very much the way wheat is steamed and cracked to make bulgur. It cooks more quickly than whole millet and is commonly steamed over a specially seasoned stew in a *couscoussier*— a pot similar to a double boiler that has a sieve as its upper pan.

Meal

Whole millet groats are sometimes coarsely ground into meal. You can use millet meal much as you would cornmeal; it has a pale color similar to white cornmeal and gives its own distinctive flavor to baked goods.

Flour

Millet flour is more finely ground than millet meal, but is somewhat coarser than white wheat flour. It lacks gluten, so must be mixed with gluten-rich flour when making yeast-raised bread. You can use it as you would corn flour.

MILLET RECIPES

Basic Steamed Millet Groats

Whole millet groats triple in volume when they are steamed.

The exact proportion of water to grain and the length of the cooking time will vary somewhat in each individual kitchen—the size and weight of the pan, the intensity of the flame, and the desired degree of softness all influence the results. The directions that follow are for grains that are cooked but discrete; if you wish to make a creamy porridge, increase both the amount of water and the cooking time.

Place 1 part whole millet groats and 2 to 3 parts water in a saucepan. Bring to a boil, cover, reduce the heat, and simmer for 20 to 30 minutes. (Millet is tasty when it is slightly sticky, but you will have to decide how it will work best in a particular recipe.)

Fluff the cooked millet with a fork and serve with butter, yogurt, or soy sauce, or use in recipes calling for cooked whole millet. You can use this basic recipe as a guide when adding millet to soup.

Millet Apple Muffins (right) will sparkle invitingly if sprinkled with a little sugar before they go into the oven.

Millet Apple Muffins

These muffins have the grainy texture of corn muffins but are not as crumbly. They are pleasantly moist and the apple-millet combination is deliciously fresh.

1	cup millet meal or flour
1	cup all-purpose flour
2	teaspoons baking powder
½	teaspoon salt
1	egg, beaten
1	cup milk
2	tablespoons honey, melted with 4 tablespoons butter, then cooled slightly
1	McIntosh apple, cored and cut into small pieces (peeled if desired)

Preheat oven to 425°F.

Mix all the dry ingredients together in a bowl. Add the milk, egg, and the butter and honey and stir together with a few quick strokes of a fork. Spoon the mixture into greased or paper-lined muffin tins. Put in preheated oven and immediately lower the temperature to 400°F. Bake for about 20 minutes, until nicely risen and golden brown on top.

Remove the muffins from the baking tins as soon as you can loosen them without breaking; this allows any remaining steam to escape and prevents them from getting soggy.

Makes ten to twelve 2-inch muffins.

Millet Pilaf with Shrimp, Fish, and Zucchini

For the seafood and marinade:

4 tablespoons chopped fresh coriander

4 tablespoons olive oil

Grated rind of 1 lemon

4 plum tomatoes, mashed with a spoon (canned are fine)

1 pound monkfish or other fleshy white fish, cut into 1-inch chunks

1 pound medium shrimp, shelled and deveined

4 medium zucchini

For the millet:

1 tablespoon olive oil

1 onion, peeled and chopped

1 cup millet

3 cups boiling water

Juice of 1 lemon

1½ tablespoons chopped fresh coriander

1 teaspoon cumin seed, crushed

Combine all the marinade ingredients in a mixing bowl, stir in the fish and shrimp, then cover and refrigerate for at least 1 hour. When you are ready to begin cooking the millet, remove the sea-

food from the refrigerator so that it can reach room temperature.

Heat the oil in a large skillet over low heat, add the onion, and sauté for 3 to 5 minutes. Add the millet and stir to coat all the grains with oil; continue to cook for 2 to 3 minutes. Add the boiling water, lemon juice, coriander, and cumin seed, and stir well to mix. Cover tightly and cook over low heat until the liquid is absorbed, about 30 minutes.

Meanwhile, preheat the oven to 450°F. Cut the zucchini lengthwise into quarters and then into ¾-inch chunks. Toss it in with the seafood.

When the millet is done, remove it from the heat but keep covered so it stays warm. Place the seafood and zucchini with their marinade juices in a baking dish and cook in the oven for about 5 minutes. Add the millet to the seafood, mixing well. Serve at once.

Makes 4 servings (double the recipe as desired to serve more diners).

Millet Bread

This lovely pale-golden bread, flavored with just a hint of cinnamon, is sturdy without being heavy. It is a good choice for toast or sandwiches. If you like, you can add raisins in the second kneading.

1 cup millet flour or meal

1 teaspoon cinnamon

1 cup water

1 package yeast (cake or fresh)

2 cups very warm water

2 tablespoons honey

1 teaspoon salt

3 tablespoons mild-flavored oil

6 to **7** cups all-purpose flour

Dissolve the millet flour and cinnamon in 1 cup of water in a saucepan and cook over low heat for about 5 minutes, stirring constantly, until the water is absorbed and the mixture thickens into a paste. Remove from the heat and let cool to room temperature.

Meanwhile, dissolve the yeast in the warm water in a large mixing bowl. Gently stir in the honey. Let the mixture

Coriander- and lemon-suffused Millet Pilaf with Shrimp, Fish, and Zucchini (left) is an enticing and simple-to-prepare main course. Marinate the sea-food ahead of time, then prepare the millet about 45 minutes before you wish to dine.

rest for about 10 minutes, until the yeast begins to bubble. Stir in the salt and oil. Add the millet mixture and stir gently until the yeast is completely dissolved. One cup at a time, stir in 6 cups of flour. Turn the dough onto a floured pastry board and knead until smooth and elastic, working in more flour as necessary. Shape the dough into a ball.

Oil a large bowl; place the dough in the bowl, turning it once to oil the top. Cover with a damp cloth and put in a warm place. Allow to rise until doubled in size, 1 to 1½ hours.

Punch the dough down and knead it briefly on the floured board. Divide into 2 pieces and let them rest while you oil 2 loaf pans. Shape the dough into loaves and place them in the pans. Rub a little oil on your hands and pat the tops of the loaves. Cover with a damp cloth and put in a warm place to rise until nearly doubled in size, about 1 hour. Preheat oven to 375°F. When ready, bake for 45 minutes. Remove from the pans to cool.

Makes 2 loaves.

Eggless Millet Brunch Pudding

This is an unusual and wonderful treat that derives its sweet taste not from sugar but from the fruit or squash with which it is made. Serve it warm from the oven, or if you are one of those people who likes cold rice pudding, try this dish as a cold summer dessert. While it needs no embellishment, you certainly won't ruin it if you add yogurt, cream, maple syrup, or more fresh fruit.

1   *cup millet*

1   *to **2** tablespoons sweet butter (more if desired)*

2   *cups total of 1 or more of the following, seeded and peeled if appropriate and cut into ½-inch chunks: winter squash (pumpkin, acorn, or butternut), apples, peaches, blueberries*

1   *tablespoon molasses, honey, or brown sugar*

2   *cups milk*

½   *teaspoon nutmeg*

If you have a covered 2-quart ovenproof and flameproof casserole, use it throughout—otherwise, start this recipe in a heavy saucepan and transfer to a casserole before baking.

Heat the casserole over medium heat. Add the millet and stir until the golden color begins to deepen. Turn the millet onto a plate or bowl and set aside.

Melt the butter in the casserole over very low heat. Stir in the squash and/or fruit and cook, stirring frequently, until it begins to soften, about 5 to 8 minutes. Next, add the molasses and honey or brown sugar and stir to dissolve. Stir in the milk and nutmeg. Raise the heat and bring the milk to the boiling point, then stir in the millet.

Preheat the oven to 325°F.

Cover the casserole and reduce the heat. Simmer without stirring for 10 to 15 minutes, until the millet has absorbed most, but not all, of the milk. Put the covered casserole in the oven and bake until the milk is completely absorbed, 20 to 30 minutes.

Fluff the mixture with a fork and serve. If you want to make an attractive presentation, mold a serving at a time in a ramekin or small bowl, then invert on a plate and garnish with yogurt, roasted nuts, or fresh fruit or drizzle with honey as appropriate.

Makes 4 servings.

Note: You can use any pie-type fruit that seems appealing in this recipe. Adjust the spices and amount of sweetener as needed (for example, cranberries would be tasty on their own or with the squash or apples, but the recipe would then require additional sugar).

Whole millet (above right) is the traditional grain for the spicy North African stew known as couscous.

Couscous

Couscous is a spicy North African stew. It is traditionally prepared in a *couscoussier* (see page 38), and the grain is steamed over the stew simmering in the bottom of the pot. You can fashion a reasonable alternative to a *couscoussier* if you have a sieve or colander that is close in size to your double boiler. Just wrap it with a tea towel so that it makes a tight fit with both the pan and lid.

The stew used for couscous can be all vegetable or include lamb or chicken.

You can prepare this dish with semolina couscous (pasta). Refer to the note that follows the recipe for an alternate preparation method.

© Tim Gibson/Envision

2	cups whole or cracked millet
2	cups water
¼	cup olive oil
2	onions, sliced
2	pounds boneless lamb, cut into 1½-inch chunks
1	teaspoon cayenne pepper
1	teaspoon ground coriander
1	teaspoon cinnamon
¼	teaspoon saffron (or 6 threads), optional
1	quart broth or water (or as needed)
3	carrots, sliced
1	small turnip, peeled and cubed
4	tomatoes, chopped
½	cup chick-peas, cooked or canned
½	cup fava beans, cooked or canned
1	zucchini, cubed
1	yellow summer squash, cubed
½	head cabbage, sliced
½	cup raisins

Combine the millet and 2 cups of water in a saucepan. (If using whole millet, bring to a boil, cover, and remove from the heat.) Let stand while you prepare and begin to cook the stew.

Heat the oil in the bottom of the *couscoussier* (or your adapted double boiler) over medium heat. Add the onion and sauté until wilted, about 5 minutes. Add the lamb and cook until it begins to brown, about 15 minutes. Sprinkle with the spices (if using saffron threads dissolve them in a couple of tablespoons of broth), and stir to mix. Add enough broth or water to cover the meat, stir, cover the pan, and bring to a boil. Reduce the heat and simmer until the meat is tender, about 1 hour.

Add the vegetables (and more broth if necessary) to the stew. If necessary, drain the millet and put it in the top of the *couscoussier* over the stew. Cover and steam for 30 minutes.

Stir in the raisins, correct the seasonings, and cook for 10 minutes longer.

Heap the millet onto a serving platter. Make a depression in the center and spoon the stew into it.

Makes 8 to 10 servings.

Note: If using semolina couscous, moisten with cold water and toss with your fingers to break up any lumps. Add to the top of the *couscoussier* and begin to steam over the stew after the lamb has been cooking for 30 minutes. After steaming for 30 minutes, transfer the couscous to a bowl, sprinkle with cold water, and toss again. Return to the *couscoussier* and finish cooking.

Very little is known about the origin of oats. They seem to have grown wild several thousand years ago in diverse parts of the world. They grow particularly well in cool, damp climates, hence their large place in Scottish cuisine. Today they are a very important crop worldwide, but, like corn, most of the harvest is used as animal fodder.

Oats are very good for humans. They are available in several forms, all of equal nutritional value (except the bran when it is isolated from the rest of the grain). When oats are processed they are simply cut and pressed or ground; none of the nutrition-rich matter is removed. Oats contain protein, B vitamins, vitamin E, and calcium, iron, and other minerals. The bran is rich in soluble fiber and there is some evidence that it can help to reduce cholesterol levels in the blood.

Oats have a sweet, nutty flavor, and we seem to prefer them at breakfast and in breads or desserts rather than in main dishes. The Scots, however, use them in many ways, and the whole groats can be used as a base for salads and stuffings.

When making sweets, complement oats with sugar, honey, molasses, raisins, fruit, cinnamon, nutmeg, and ginger—and butter and cream. When using them in savory dishes, add celery, carrots, onions, nuts, mild herbs such as thyme and parsley, and cheese, eggs, and milk if desired.

© Lynn Karlin

Oat Groats

Steel-cut Oats

Rolled Oats

Groats

Oat groats are whole kernels that have been lightly toasted so that the two inedible protective outer layers of the hull can be easily removed. This heating process lends a slightly roasted flavor to oats and also deactivates an enzyme that might otherwise impart a soapy taste.

Oat groats can be cooked whole like rice. They can be added to breads like wheat berries. They can be sprouted and of course can be eaten as porridge; they taste somewhat different from the usual oatmeal.

Steel-cut

Steel-cut oats are whole oat groats that have been sliced lengthwise into several pieces. They are sometimes called Scotch oats, and come in several grades. The more finely they are sliced, the faster they cook. They can be prepared as porridge, but they take about an hour to cook.

Rolled (Old-fashioned and Quick-cooking)

Old-fashioned rolled oats are made from groats that have been steamed so that they are soft, and then passed between rollers so they are flat. Quick-cooking oats are made in the same way, but the groats are sliced before they are steamed. Quick-cooking oats cook faster than the old-fashioned variety, but both are quite quick to prepare. Instant oatmeal is made from groats that have been cooked and then flattened. Although it has more or less the same nutritional value as other forms of oats, instant oatmeal is usually packaged with salt and sugar, so read the labels to be sure you want to eat it.

Oats—delicate grains with a delicate and delicious flavor—do not lose their nutritional value through processing on the way from field (left) to store.

Oat Flour

Flour

Oat flour is finely ground whole oat groats. It is sweet and white, but contains no gluten. It adds a wonderful flavor to all baked goods, although it must be mixed with gluten-rich flours when making yeast-raised bread. Quick breads and pastries are delightful when some or all of the wheat flour is replaced with oat flour.

Oat Bran

Bran

Oat bran is the layer that covers the whole groat under the inedible hull. It is rich in fiber and may help to lower blood cholesterol. It can be added to baked goods or granola, or sprinkled on cereal or yogurt.

OAT RECIPES

Basic Steamed Oat Groats

Whole oat groats triple in volume when they are steamed.

The exact proportion of water to grain and the length of the cooking time will vary somewhat in each individual kitchen—the size and weight of the pan, the intensity of the flame, and the desired degree of softness all influence the results. The directions that follow are for grains that are cooked but discrete (steamed oats never really get dry); if you wish to make a creamy porridge, increase both the amount of water and the cooking time.

Place 1 part whole oat groats and a little less than 2 parts water in a saucepan. Bring to a boil, cover, reduce the heat, and simmer for 40 minutes. Oats can also be cooked in milk; cook them in the top of a double boiler over boiling water and allow a little more time for them to absorb the milk.

Fluff the cooked oats with a fork and serve with butter or yogurt, or use in recipes calling for cooked whole oats. You can use this basic recipe as a guide when adding oats to soup.

How To Make Oatmeal

How creamy do you like your oatmeal? The method you use to prepare it, as well as the ratio of water to oats, will affect its texture. Allow at least one-third cup uncooked rolled oats per serving and prepare by one of the following methods. Serve oatmeal with milk or yogurt, honey or brown sugar, cinnamon or nutmeg, and raisins or fruit. If you like the raisins hot, plump, and juicy, cook them along with the oats.

Basic Oatmeal

Use 2 parts water to 1 part rolled oats, plus ¼ teaspoon salt (or to taste) for every cup of oats. For *creamy* oatmeal, bring the water and salt to a boil, stir in the rolled oats, and cook for about 5 minutes over medium-low heat, stirring once or twice. Then cover the pan, remove from the heat, and let stand 15 to 20 minutes. For *extra creamy* oatmeal, place the oats in cold water and follow the same procedure. For *even creamier* oatmeal, follow the directions for steel-cut oats below. For *less creamy* oatmeal, boil the oats for 2 to 3 minutes and let stand 10 to 15 minutes.

Textured (Non-creamy) Oatmeal

Use 1½ parts water to 1 part rolled oats, plus ¼ teaspoon salt (or to taste) for every cup of oats. Bring the water and salt to a boil, stir in the oatmeal, cover the pan, remove from the heat, and let stand for 3 to 5 minutes.

Steel-cut oatmeal (above right) complemented with a garnish of fresh raspberries.

© Burke/Triolo

Steel-cut Oatmeal

Steel-cut oats take longer to cook, but make a lovely creamy porridge. For best results, soak them overnight and cook them in a double boiler so they do not stick or scorch. Use 4 parts water to 1 part steel-cut oats (3 parts water to 1 part rolled oats), plus ¼ teaspoon salt (or to taste) for each cup of oats. Combine the ingredients in the top of a double boiler and refrigerate the mixture overnight. Place over boiling water, cover, and steam gently for 30 minutes to 1 hour, stirring occasionally, until the oats reach the consistency you prefer.

Light-as-Air Oat Scones make wonderful tea cakes. Try them as a fruit shortcake dessert in summer as well.

Light-as-Air Oat Flour Scones

The oat flour lends a natural sweetness to these pretty tea cakes. They are very light and a little crumbly. If you like, serve them warm, topped with butter and jam.

1   cup oat flour
2   teaspoons baking powder
1   tablespoon sugar
    Pinch of salt
    Dash of nutmeg (one shake of the container)
4   tablespoons butter
1   egg
2   tablespoons milk

Preheat oven to 350°F.

Mix all the dry ingredients together in a bowl. Cut in the butter with a pastry blender until pea-size. Beat the egg together with the milk and add to the dry ingredients. Using a fork, mix together with a few quick strokes. Turn the dough onto a lightly floured board. Knead gently for a few moments, then roll or pat into a ½-inch-thick round. Cut into 6 pie-shape wedges. Place the wedges about ½-inch apart on a cookie sheet and bake in preheated oven for 15 minutes.

Makes 6 scones.

Creamy Oat Soup with Fennel

Serve this as an unusual first course or luncheon entrée. It can be made very quickly, but the flavors will meld delightfully if you let it sit for at least an hour before serving. If you do not have fresh fennel, substitute celery and add 1 teaspoon crushed fennel seed, or change the flavor completely by using celery and seasoning the soup with fresh dill.

1   tablespoon butter
½   cup thinly sliced fennel bulb
1   small leek, cleaned and thinly sliced
1   shallot, peeled and thinly sliced
     Pinch of fresh thyme
1   cup chicken stock (if canned, use ½ cup stock and ½ cup water)
1   cup milk
1   cup cooked whole oat groats
     Salt and freshly ground pepper (to taste)

Melt the butter over low heat in a heavy saucepan. Cook the fennel, leek, shallot, and thyme for 10 minutes, stirring occasionally. Stir in the stock and milk and heat to the simmering point. Stir in the oats, cover, and simmer for 10 minutes. If time permits, remove the soup from the heat and let stand for 1 hour, then return to the simmering point before serving. Season with salt and pepper.

Makes 4 servings.

Note: You can substitute uncooked rolled oats for the cooked oat groats, but add ½ cup liquid to the soup.

© Burke/Triolo

Oat Flour Apple Tart

This is perhaps the easiest and most foolproof tart you will ever make. The crust is a variation on a French *pâte sucrée* (sweet crust), and requires no special handling. The egg keeps it from getting soggy. The oat flavor is particularly nice with tart apples like McIntosh or Granny Smith, but is also good with blueberries, peaches, plums, or whatever fruit is in season. If possible, bake this in a fluted tart pan with a removable bottom. It can be served warm or at room temperature.

For the crust (makes two 9-inch crusts):

1   cup oat flour
1   cup white flour
⅓   cup sugar
2   pinches salt
8   tablespoons butter
1   egg

For the filling (makes one 9-inch tart):
3   to **4** firm, slightly tart apples, peeled, quartered, cored, and cut into slices
     Sugar
     Nutmeg
     Milk

Sift all the dry ingredients for the crust together onto a pastry board. Pound the butter with the side of a rolling pin to soften. Make a well in the middle of the flour and break the egg into it. Stir the egg with your fingers to break it up; draw in just a little of the flour. Add the pounded butter to the egg and work together with your fingers. Gradually work the flour into the egg/butter mixture, making a firm but pliable dough (like a

Oat Flour Apple Tart (right) easy, foolproof, and divine.

roll-out cookie dough). Divide the dough into 2 balls, flatten them slightly, and wrap in wax paper. Refrigerate for at least 1 hour; you can freeze a ball if you do not want to bake 2 tarts.

Roll the dough into a round on the floured board. Try to roll it so that it is just barely bigger than the diameter plus twice the depth of your pan. Roll the dough up on your rolling pin, then unroll it over the tart pan. Gently settle the dough into the pan up against the sides, folding any extra over the top edge. Roll the rolling pin around the top of the pan, pressing hard enough to cut off the excess dough.

Preheat oven to 350°F.

Arrange the apple slices in an attractive pattern in the tart shell (it doesn't have to be perfect to be attractive). Sprinkle with the least possible amount of sugar and a little nutmeg. Bake in preheated oven for 30 minutes, then brush the apples with a little milk. If the tart seems to be browning too quickly, lay a piece of foil loosely over it. Bake for another 15 minutes.

The crust will separate from the sides of the pan while baking. If you have used a pie pan with a removable bottom, place the tart on a plate before serving.

Makes 2 tarts.

Classic Shortbread

Here is the cookie that is perfect for afternoon tea and quick enough to make for unexpected guests. Let it cool before serving—shortbread is fragile and less flavorful when warm.

12	*tablespoons sweet butter*
½	*cup sugar*
1¼	*cups all-purpose flour*
¾	*cups oat flour*
	Grated rind of 1 lemon
18	*pecan halves, coarsely broken*

Preheat oven to 325°F.

Cream the butter and sugar in a mixing bowl. Dust the surface of your pastry board with 2 tablespoons of the all-purpose flour. Mix the rest with the oat flour, lemon rind, and pecans. Add to the butter and sugar and mix well, kneading with your fingers if necessary. Gather the dough into a ball, roll it on the floured board to coat, then flatten and pat or roll into a ⅜-inch-thick rectangle. To make your cookies extra-attractive, trim the edges of the rectangle with a sharp knife. Cut the dough into 1- by 2-inch bars and place on an ungreased cookie sheet. Bake in preheated oven until golden at the edges, about 20 minutes. Transfer to a wire rack to cool.

Makes two dozen 1- by 2-inch cookies.

Variations:

Herbed Shortbread: Substitute 2 tablespoons chopped fresh rosemary or hyssop leaves or 2 teaspoons crushed fennel or aniseed for the pecans.

Chocolate-studded Shortbread: Substitute walnuts for the pecans and add 1 ounce very coarsely chopped bittersweet chocolate.

Fruited Shortbread: Substitute raisins or chopped candied citron for the pecans.

Classic Shortbread can be cut in any shape desired; pie wedges are traditional.

Spiced Oatmeal Drop Cookies

Easy to make and much too easy to consume in large quantities, these cookies (right) are firm and slightly chewy. They keep well and have a habit of going down with the breakfast coffee. They can be made by any child strong enough to cream the butter and old enough to read the measuring spoon. Don't overbake; they should just begin to turn brown.

½	*cup butter*
¾	*cup sugar or ½ cup honey*
1	*egg, beaten*
⅓	*cup milk*
1¾	*cups rolled oats*
½	*cup raisins or chocolate chips (optional)*
½	*cup chopped walnuts (optional)*
1½	*cups all-purpose flour*
½	*teaspoon salt*
½	*teaspoon baking soda*
½	*teaspoon cinnamon*
½	*teaspoon ground cloves*
½	*teaspoon nutmeg*

Preheat oven to 375°F.

Cream the butter in a large mixing bowl. Add the sugar or honey and mix well. Whisk in the egg and beat until fluffy. Beat in the milk. Mix the rolled oats with the raisins or chocolate chips and nuts, if using, and stir into the butter mixture. Mix the flour with the salt, baking soda, and spices, and stir into the butter and oats, mixing very thoroughly.

Drop by the teaspoonful, ½ inch apart, on greased cookie sheets and bake in preheated oven for about 15 minutes. Transfer to a wire rack to cool.

Makes four to five dozen 1-inch cookies.

Oatmeal Topping for Fruit Cobblers

When you are not feeling up to making pie crust, or if you've got a particularly "soggy" fruit like rhubarb, try this cobbler topping. It can be mixed together in just a few minutes and takes on a lovely added flavor from the juices of whatever fruit you use as they bubble up into it while baking. Adjust the spices as appropriate to the fruit.

You can bake a cobbler in a regular pie pan, but it's nice to use a fairly deep baking dish if you have one, so that both the fruit and topping can be layered in generously.

For the topping:

1	cup flour (oat or all-purpose)
½	cup rolled oats
½	cup sugar
1	teaspoon baking powder
¼	teaspoon salt (optional)
2	shakes of the nutmeg can (or to taste)
6	tablespoons cold butter

For the filling:

Fruit of your choice, peeled and cut into chunks as appropriate, enough to fill 9-inch pie pan

Grated rind of 1 lemon

Sugar as appropriate (most fruit requires very little sugar)

Spice if desired

1	egg, beaten (optional)

Preheat oven to 375°F.

Place all of the topping ingredients except the butter in a mixing bowl and mix with a fork until well blended. Cut in the butter; it should be pea-size and well-coated with the dry ingredients.

Mix the filling in the pie pan (the egg helps to firm up the fruit juices; if you choose not to use it, the cobbler will be a bit more runny but just as good). Sprinkle the topping over the fruit, making a layer about ½ inch thick. Place the baking dish on a cookie sheet to protect your oven from bubbly spills, and bake in preheated oven until the topping is golden, about 45 minutes.

Makes more than enough to top a 9-inch pie, depending upon how thickly you use it.

Note: This is one recipe where honey or molasses simply won't work the same way as sugar. If you make a substitution, the topping will not be as crispy-crunchy.

Oat Flour Bread

Bake this bread in regular loaf pans or 6- to 7-inch-diameter casseroles.

1	cup oat flour
2	cups whole-wheat flour
1¾	cups all-purpose flour
½	teaspoon salt
1	package yeast (cake or fresh)
1¾	cups warm water
1	tablespoon honey
½	cup toasted rolled oats or cooked wheat berries or raisins or walnut pieces

Place all three flours and the salt in a large mixing bowl. Mix together and make a deep well in the center. Place the yeast in the well, pour ½ cup of the warm water over it, add the honey, and stir gently. Stir in just a bit of the flour and let the mixture rest for about 10 minutes until the yeast begins to bubble. Slowly add the remaining water and gradually stir in the rest of the flour to make a soft, slightly sticky dough.

Dust a pastry board with oat flour. Turn the dough onto board. Knead until smooth and elastic. Oil a large bowl; place dough in bowl, turning once to oil the top. Cover with a damp cloth and put in a warm place. Allow to rise until doubled in size, 1 to 1½ hours.

Punch dough down and return to the board. Knead in oats, berries, raisins, or walnuts. Divide in half, put in oiled baking pans, cover, and let rise until doubled in size, about 30 minutes.

Preheat the oven to 400°F. Put the pans in the oven and lower the temperature to 375°F. Bake for 45 minutes.

Makes 2 loaves.

QUINOA

1980s and began to test-grow it in Colorado. It is now available (at premium prices) in health-food stores and specialty markets, where you may find it in pasta, snacks, and cereals as well as whole and as flour.

Quinoa is very nutritious. It is high in protein (with all of the essential amino acids) and important vitamins and minerals as well as starch, sugar, and fat. It is the nature of quinoa's protein that has led to all the superlatives.

Quinoa has a smoky sesamelike taste. When ground into flour, it takes on a slightly bitter but not unpleasant flavor. The ivory-colored grains are small, flat, and round, and are ringed by the germ. When the seeds are cooked they become translucent and the germ band pulls away slightly; they are delicate, pretty, and seem very "light" for a carbohydrate. Quinoa is as versatile as rice or millet, but it seems a shame to overwhelm its subtle flavor with heavily seasoned sauces. Complement quinoa with scallions, dill, chicken, seafood, citrus flavors, vinaigrette, or soy sauce. Baked goods that are made with quinoa flour can be savory or sweet and lightly spiced.

Q uinoa has been called "the super grain" and "the grain of the nineties." Quinoa is a relative of the common garden weed lamb's-quarters. It grows quite tall and has a bushy head of seeds. Like amaranth and buckwheat, it is not a grass but it takes its culinary place among the grains.

Quinoa came originally from the Andes in South America, where it was cultivated by the Incas, who referred to it as the mother grain. After the Spanish conquests of the sixteenth century, it became a minor crop and was not commonly known until recently. Two Americans learned of quinoa in the

Tiny, nutrition-packed quinoa, while expensive as grains go, is well worth discovering and serving for special occasions.

WHAT TO LOOK FOR IN THE MARKET

Whole Quinoa Seeds

Whole Quinoa Seeds

Quinoa seeds are similar in appearance to millet, but are distinguished by the germ band that surrounds their perimeter. The seeds are naturally coated with bitter-tasting saponins that protect them from birds and insects. When they are harvested, the saponins are removed by washing or rubbing. The seeds should be rinsed thoroughly before cooking.

Quinoa can be eaten on its own as a hot cereal (good for small fry) or side dish, and can be used in soups, salads, casseroles, pilafs, and desserts. Because it cooks very quickly and is so light on the palate, it is an excellent choice for a summer grain. It can also be sprouted; let the sprouts green before adding them to salads.

Flour

Quinoa flour is ground from whole quinoa seeds and imparts a pleasant and delicate flavor to baked goods. It can also be boiled in water to make an infant cereal. Because quinoa is not refined nor is its germ removed before it is ground, the naturally occurring oils in the seeds can turn rancid. The flour should be refrigerated and is best used within six months.

QUINOA RECIPES

Basic Steamed Quinoa

Whole quinoa nearly triples in volume when steamed.

The exact proportion of water to grain and the length of the cooking time will vary somewhat in each individual kitchen—the size and weight of the pan, the intensity of the flame, and the desired degree of softness all influence the results. The directions that follow are for grains that are cooked but discrete; if you wish to make a creamy porridge, increase both the amount of water and the cooking time.

Place 1 part whole quinoa seeds and 2 parts water in a saucepan. Bring to a boil, cover, reduce the heat, and simmer for 12 to 15 minutes.

Fluff the cooked quinoa with a fork and serve with butter, yogurt, or soy sauce, or use in recipes calling for cooked whole quinoa. You can use this basic recipe as a guide when adding quinoa to soup.

Quinoa Watercress Salad

Serve this on a bed of greens with ripe tomato wedges for a lovely summer lunch. Add diced cooked chicken if you like. Combine the ingredients just before serving so the watercress does not get soggy.

For the salad:
2 *cups cooked quinoa*
1 *bunch watercress, washed and coarsely chopped*
1 *stalk celery, finely diced*
¼ *cup chopped scallions (include some of the green part)*
½ *cup broken walnut meats*
2 *ounces Roquefort cheese, crumbled Salt and freshly ground pepper (to taste)*

For the dressing:
1 *to 2 teaspoons prepared Dijon mustard*
2 *tablespoons balsamic vinegar*
4 *tablespoons olive or walnut oil*

Combine all the salad ingredients in a bowl. Mix the dressing by dissolving the mustard in the vinegar, then adding the oil. Add to the salad to taste—you probably won't need it all.

Makes 2 main servings or 4 side servings.

Quinoa Watercress Salad (right) has an unusual blend of smokey, tart, and salty flavors.

Quinoa Vegetable Skillet Cake

Here is a tasty—and very simple to prepare—side dish or vegetarian entrée that falls somewhere between a classic potato pancake and a French vegetable *tian*. It can be baked in the oven or, if you wish, spooned onto a griddle and fried like croquettes. The vegetable taste of quinoa is particularly nice with the suggested ingredients; if you are an adventurous chef, you will no doubt be able to come up with infinite variations on this theme.

1½ cups cooked quinoa
1 tart apple, cored and finely chopped
1 onion, grated
1 carrot, grated
1 cup steamed and drained chopped spinach (frozen is fine)
  Grated rind of 1 lemon or orange
⅓ cup quinoa flour (or all-purpose)
¼ teaspoon baking soda
¼ teaspoon cumin seed, crushed or ground
¼ teaspoon cinnamon
¼ cup yogurt
  Juice of 1 lemon or orange
1 egg or 2 egg whites
  Salt and freshly ground pepper (to taste)
  Small amount of oil to lubricate pan

In a large mixing bowl, mix the quinoa, apple, onion, carrot, spinach, and lemon or orange rind. Measure the flour, and while it is still in the measuring cup blend in the baking soda and spices. Add to the quinoa mixture and stir together until well mixed. Measure the yogurt, and while it is still in the measuring cup add the lemon or orange juice and egg and beat briefly to mix. Add to the quinoa mixture and stir together until well mixed. Season with salt and pepper.

Preheat the oven to 375°F.

Lightly oil a 10-inch skillet or pie pan. Press the quinoa mixture into the pan and bake until it begins to brown and pull away from the sides, about 25 minutes. Or, heat and oil a griddle and drop spoonfuls of the quinoa mixture onto it, flattening each into a patty about 4 inches in diameter and ½ inch thick. Cook for about 5 minutes on each side; you will probably have to oil the griddle frequently.

Serve topped with yogurt (season with lemon juice, pepper, and chopped scallion if desired).

Makes one 10-inch pie; serves 4 as a side dish, 2 as an entrée.

Quinoa Pecan Waffles

Quinoa flour has a slight vegetable taste that gives these waffles a subtle flavor.

½ cup quinoa flour
½ cup all-purpose flour
¼ cup pecan meats, broken into small pieces
1½ teaspoons baking powder
¼ teaspoon salt
1 cup milk
1 egg
1 tablespoon vegetable oil

Mix all the dry ingredients together in a bowl and make a well in the center. Beat the milk, egg, and oil together. Add to the dry ingredients and stir until well blended. Fill the waffle iron with some of the batter and cook following the manufacturer's directions.

Makes 5 to 6 waffles; double the recipe as you like.

Quinoa Vegetable Skillet Cake, cooked in patties (left).

Quinoa with Mussels and Tuna

This dish is similar to paella. The smoky flavor of the seafood is a pleasant complement to the delicate grain.

For the marinade:

1	tablespoon mild-flavored vegetable oil
2	tablespoons chopped fresh coriander leaves
	Juice of 1 lemon
	Freshly ground pepper

For the seafood:

1½	pounds fresh tuna, cut in 1-inch cubes
1	tablespoon mild oil
1	medium leek, white part only, cleaned and thinly sliced
2	large shallots, thinly sliced
3	cups water
3	pounds mussels, scrubbed and debearded
2	cups quinoa, rinsed
1	medium red bell pepper, seeded and diced
1	cup fresh petits pois or 1 package frozen

Mix the marinade in a bowl large enough to hold the tuna. Coat the tuna in the marinade; cover and refrigerate for several hours.

Heat the oil in a large, heavy saucepan or Dutch oven. Add the leek and shallots, stir to coat, cover, and cook over a low heat until limp, about 10 minutes. Stir in the tuna with the marinade and

cook, covered, for 10 minutes, stirring occasionally to prevent sticking. Leaving as much of the cooking liquid as possible, remove the tuna from the pan, cover, and set aside.

Pour about 1 inch of water into the bottom of the pan. Cover and bring to a boil over a high heat. Add the mussels and steam them for about 8 minutes, until the shells begin to open. Remove the mussels with a slotted spoon, cover, and set aside.

Add the quinoa to the cooking liquid along with the remainder of the water. Stir once, cover, lower the heat, and cook for about 10 minutes. Check for tenderness and add more water if necessary; continue to cook until the quinoa is nearly done.

Preheat oven to 375°F.

If your cooking pan is not large enough to hold all of the ingredients with room to spare, or if it is not oven-proof, transfer the quinoa and any remaining liquid to a large baking dish. Stir in the bell pepper and petits pois. Stir in the tuna and mussels. Cover, using foil if necessary, and place in preheated oven for 5 to 8 minutes, until all the ingredients are hot. If the quinoa is tender and cooking liquid remains in the dish, remove the cover and cook a few minutes longer. Serve immediately.

Makes 6 to 8 servings.

Quinoa Carrot Quick Bread

The unusual flavor of quinoa flour makes this moist loaf a special alternative to corn bread. Here is a basic recipe—you can experiment with seasonings to suit the occasion for which you wish to serve it. For a sweeter breakfast or tea bread, double the honey and add raisins, some cinnamon, ginger, or other spice. For a savory bread to accompany soup or a main meal, try adding a generous pinch of dill, thyme, or even chopped onion, and a twist of freshly ground pepper.

1	cup quinoa flour
1	cup all-purpose flour
½	teaspoon salt
3	teaspoons baking powder
½	cup cooked quinoa
1	grated carrot
1	cup milk
1	egg, beaten
2	tablespoons honey, melted in 5 tablespoons butter, cooled slightly

Preheat oven to 375°F.

Mix all the dry ingredients together in a bowl. Add the cooked quinoa and carrot and stir well to coat with the flour. Add the milk, egg, and the butter and honey and stir together with a few quick strokes of a fork. Spoon the mixture into greased loaf pan. Bake in preheated oven until done, about 45 minutes. Let cool for 10 minutes and remove from the pan.

Makes 1 loaf.

Farmers tending the rice fields in the Philippines.

For over half of the world's population, rice is *the* staple food; for some it is the only source of protein. Rice is a native of Asia, perhaps specifically of India, and came (via shipwreck) to the New World in the seventeenth century. Rice plants must be submerged for much of their growing period, and thrive in warm, moist climates.

Rice, like wheat and barley, is a grain that is all too often eaten in a highly refined, less nourishing state. Most of its nutrients are in the bran layer that surrounds each kernel. Unfortunately, most of the people for whom rice is a primary food are guilty of consuming it with much of its value milled away. Rice is easily digested, contains very little fat or sodium, and has no gluten, so it is a good carbohydrate choice for people on restrictive diets. When eaten in its less refined forms, it is a good source of protein, vitamins, and minerals. Rice is also used to make vinegar, beer, and wine.

Many people think of rice simply as a filling carrier for meats, vegetables, and sauces, but the nutty flavor of brown rice can enhance a dish or stand on its own—and provide nourishment. The more exotic wild and basmati rices have unique flavors that make special contributions to a meal. More importantly, the flavor of rice seems to be enhanced by the seasonings in which it is cooked, and this may account for its frequent appearances in diverse cuisines.

Your imagination is the limit when seasoning rice. The flavor of the different varieties ranges from pleasantly mild to nutty. It can be incorporated into virtually any cuisine, from classic Continental to exotic Asian. Complement it with sweet, savory, or spicy seasonings, serve it plain or fancy, mix it with meats, poultry, fish, vegetables, dairy, or fruits. In fact, the only thing rice doesn't mix with naturally is sweet chocolate.

The length of the grain. Rice is most commonly identified as long-, medium-, or short-grain. The primary difference between the three types is in their behavior when cooked, rather than in their nutritive value. *Long-grain* rice is thin, about five times as long as wide. When cooked the grains are fairly dry and fluffy, and separate well from one another. Long-grain rice is best used in soups, pilafs, and salads, or any place that you want the grains to be distinct.

Long-grain Rice

Short-grain Rice

Arborio Rice

Sweet Rice

Short-grain rice is almost round when cooked; it is glutinous and so the grains stick together, making it an ideal choice for dishes to be eaten with chopsticks. Less common ***medium-grain*** rice is more tender than long-grain rice and shares some of the sticky qualities of short-grain.

VARIETIES

Rice comes in many varieties and degrees of refinement (all varieties are brown until they are refined). Some varieties are grown in specific parts of the world and their special flavors enhance certain cuisines. While the more exotic rice does make a difference in the taste of a dish, most recipes that call for it will be quite successful made from a more common variety, should availability or budget affect your selection. Rice is often prepackaged with assorted seasonings, but if your pantry shelves are reasonably well stocked there is a nearly endless variety of interesting rice dishes that can be prepared easily from scratch. Most varieties of rice are inexpensive and keep well if stored away from pests.

Arborio rice is a pearly short-grain Italian rice that has a creamy texture when cooked. It is available at specialty-food shops and is very expensive.

Basmati Rice

Basmati rice is a type of long-grain rice that is grown in parts of India and Pakistan. It has a distinctive, somewhat sweet flavor and aroma. It is one of the only exotic rices that is readily available either brown or white.

Sushi rice is a short-grain Japanese rice that is somewhat translucent when cooked. Incidentally, rice is pickled before it is used in sushi.

Sweet rice is a waxy short-grain variety that becomes very soft when cooked. It is sometimes used to make desserts or baby cereals, and can be used to thicken sauces. In Japanese cuisine it is used cooked, worked into a paste in a mortar, cut into slabs, and fried to make *mochi* (rice cakes). Look for sweet rice in a gourmet shop or Oriental grocery.

Texmati rice is a cross between a domestic North American long-grain rice and basmati rice. As the name implies, it is grown in Texas.

Wild Rice

Wild rice is not a true rice. The grains are the seeds of a North American aquatic grass. Much of the crop is gathered by Native Americans in the Great Lakes region; it is also grown commercially in parts of the Midwest and California. Because it is rather difficult to grow and harvest it tends to be expensive; it is available in three grades, giant, extra fancy, and select, which further dictate the price.

Wild rice is never refined and is very good for you. It has a distinctive nutty flavor and as it cooks the grains pop open and curl attractively. It can be prepared on its own or mixed in with true rice; it is often eaten with game and is an excellent choice for rice salad. Wild rice can also be popped like popcorn.

WHAT TO LOOK FOR IN THE MARKET

Whole Rice Types

When rice is harvested, the grains are covered with an inedible hull and a nutrient-rich bran layer. It is refined through a process known as milling or polishing, which removes the bran, germ, and polish (a thin layer under the bran). Polished rice is almost pure starch; a diet that relies heavily on it may result in severe vitamin deficiency, so it is often enriched. However, this enrichment does not come close to replacing the nutrients that were removed. Enriched rice should not be washed before it is cooked because much of the enrichment will rinse away.

Whole rice is available in four degrees of refinement. The less refined it is, the longer it takes to cook. However, the labor involved is minimal for all types and the rest of a meal can be cooked while the rice is steaming. Rice can be prepared ahead of time if it is to be incorporated cooked into a recipe.

Brown rice is not polished; only the inedible hull and a small amount of the bran is removed. It is the most nutritious form of rice that you can eat, as it contains vitamin E and fiber, and more protein and other nutrients than polished rice. It takes a little longer than polished rice to cook and needs more water, but it has more flavor and expands to a greater quantity per volume.

Converted rice is parboiled before it is milled. This is a special steaming process that forces some of the nutrients found in the bran and germ into the starch of the grain. Although it is more nutritious than white rice, it lacks the fiber and some of the protein of brown rice. If you feel that a recipe will benefit from the taste of polished rice, enriched converted rice is the healthiest choice.

White rice is whole-grain rice that has had the hull, bran, and germ polished away. It requires less cooking time than either brown or converted rice. If you eat a lot of white rice be sure to buy a brand that has been enriched.

Instant rice is precooked white rice. It is the most highly processed whole rice and the least nutritious. It is also more expensive.

Flour

Rice flour is ground from whole-rice grains (usually white). It has very little flavor, although brown-rice flour has a slightly stronger taste and is somewhat more nutritious. It is sometimes used by people who are allergic to wheat, although it has no gluten and cannot be used alone to make yeast-raised bread. It tends to produce crumbly baked goods when used alone and requires quite a bit of leavening agent (two and a half teaspoons per cup of flour); it can be used fairly successfully in recipes that include eggs. Rice flour is used to make some varieties of Oriental noodles. Look for them in specialty grocers or an Oriental market.

Rice Bran and Polishings

Rice bran and polishings are the parts of brown rice that are milled away when it is polished. Used as a natural source of vitamins, they can be added to baked goods in the same manner as wheat bran and germ.

RICE RECIPES

Basic Steamed Rice

Rice triples in volume when steamed.
The exact proportion of water to grain and the length of the cooking time will vary somewhat in each individual kitchen—the size and weight of the pan, the intensity of the flame, and the desired degree of softness all influence the results. The directions that follow are for grains that are cooked but discrete; if you wish to make a creamy porridge, increase both the amount of water and the cooking time.

Place 1 part rice to 2½ parts water in a saucepan. Bring to a boil, cover, reduce the heat. Simmer 30 to 40 minutes for brown rice; 20 minutes for converted rice; 15 minutes for white rice.

Rice can be sautéed for a few minutes in a small amount of butter or oil before it is steamed. This will add flavor and help the grains to separate.

Fluff the cooked rice with a fork and serve with butter, yogurt, or soy sauce, or use in recipes calling for cooked rice. You can use this basic recipe as a guide when adding rice to soup.

How to Cook Wild Rice

Wild rice doubles in volume when it is steamed.
Wild rice should always be rinsed thoroughly before it is cooked. It can be cooked following the directions for cooking regular rice, but allow 3 parts liquid to 1 part grain, and cook it for about 40 minutes. When it is done the grains will curl and pop open. You can cook it together with brown rice if you like. Wild rice and whole triticale can be substituted for one another in recipes as long as you allow for the difference in cooking times.

Wild rice has a nutty taste and is wonderful mixed, hot or cold, with other grains or even pasta; the wild rice flavor is fairly strong so this can be both complementary and cost-effective. If you are adventurous you can let your taste buds guide you through many experiments with it. At right wild rice is tossed into a salad with orzo (rice-shaped pasta), pine nuts, prunes, olives, and parsley; try dressing it with olive oil and fresh-squeezed lemon juice.

Wild Rice Salad with Raspberry Vinaigrette

Rice salad can be as simple or as complex as your imagination allows. This is one of the simplest, but it does contain one unusual ingredient—raspberry vinegar—that contributes an unmistakable and delicate taste.

For the salad:

1 cup cooked wild rice
1 cup cooked rice, white or brown, as desired
½ cup slivered almonds
½ cup chopped scallion, white and green parts
   Salt and freshly ground pepper (to taste)

For the vinaigrette:

3 tablespoons raspberry vinegar
6 tablespoons mild-flavored oil
   Pinch of fresh hyssop or thyme

Mix the wild and regular rice with the almonds and scallion and season with salt and pepper. Mix the raspberry vinegar, oil, and hyssop or thyme until well blended. Add the vinaigrette to the rice mixture, mix well, and refrigerate for a couple of hours to blend the flavors. Serve chilled or at room temperature.

Makes 4 servings.

Wild Rice Salad with Raspberry Vinaigrette (left). In the background is a bowl of uncooked triticale (see page 78), which can be substituted for some or all of either the wild or regular rice.

Summer Garden Rice Salad

Rice tossed with fresh vegetables in a hearty mustard dressing makes a lovely main course in summertime. All the ingredients should be at room temperature; the salad will be best if assembled just before you eat it. This recipe is just a beginning—you can vary the ingredients as you wish or add cooked chicken or cooled steamed mussels if you like.

For the salad:

2 cups cooked rice, preferably brown
1 small zucchini, diced attractively
1 small yellow summer squash, diced attractively
1 cup shelled fresh peas
1 cup string beans, steamed briefly and cut in ½-inch pieces
1 cup broccoli florets, steamed briefly if desired
1 small red bell pepper, cored and diced
   Kernels from 1 steamed ear of sweet corn
   Several fresh basil leaves, chopped
2 ripe tomatoes, diced, or 10 cherry tomatoes
   Salt and freshly ground pepper (to taste)
   Assorted salad greens to line a serving platter
½ cup black olives
¼ pound mozzarella cheese, smoked or fresh as you like, cut into small chunks

For the dressing:

1 tablespoon prepared Dijon mustard
2 tablespoons herb vinegar, preferably basil or thyme
4 tablespoons olive oil

Combine all the ingredients from the rice through the tomatoes in a large mixing bowl. Mix the dressing by dissolving the mustard in the vinegar, then adding the olive oil. Add to the rice mixture to taste—you probably won't need it all. Season with salt and pepper if desired. Make a bed of salad greens on a large platter, and arrange the rice mixture on it. Garnish with the olives and mozzarella.

Makes 6 to 8 main-dish servings.

Sweet and Sour Rice Pilaf with Lentils

This unusual pilaf tastes more complicated than it is: It takes very little more time and effort to prepare than basic rice. It is particularly tasty when made with brown rice. Depending upon the season, you can serve it hot or at room temperature. Either way is delicious. This is a dry pilaf, so it can be served with yogurt on the side if desired.

¾ cup lentils, rinsed and picked over
2½ cups water
2 cloves garlic, peeled and smashed with a rolling pin
¼ small onion, stuck with 2 cloves
2 sprigs fresh thyme
1 small sprig fresh rosemary
¾ cup walnut meats, broken
1 cup rice
2 cups water or stock
2 carrots, cleaned and diced
   Grated rind of 1 lemon
1 tablespoon honey (or to taste)
2 tablespoons balsamic vinegar (or to taste)
6 tablespoons olive oil (or to taste)
   Salt and freshly ground pepper (to taste)

Preheat oven to 375°F.

Place the lentils in a saucepan with the water. Wrap the garlic, onion, thyme, and rosemary in a piece of cheesecloth and add to the lentils. Bring the water to a boil, cover, reduce the heat, and sim-

mer until tender, about 45 minutes. Check from time to time to see that the water has not boiled away; add more liquid if necessary.

While the lentils are cooking, toast the walnut meats (on a small cookie sheet) in preheated oven for about 15 minutes, or until they begin to darken. Set aside.

Meanwhile, place the rice and water or stock in a saucepan, bring to a boil, cover, reduce the heat, and simmer until the rice is tender and the liquid absorbed, about 30 minutes. If the rice is done before the lentils, set aside and keep warm if possible.

After the lentils have cooked for about 30 minutes, add the diced carrots to the saucepan and continue to simmer. When the lentils are tender, drain and reserve the liquid. Discard the garlic, onion, and herbs. Return the lentils and about ¼ cup of their cooking liquid to the saucepan and place over a low heat. Add the lemon rind and toasted walnuts. Drain the rice (or add water) if necessary, stirring to mix. Stir in the honey, vinegar, olive oil, salt, and pepper, and mix well. Taste the pilaf and adjust the seasonings if desired.

Makes 6 to 8 side dish servings; leftovers are delicious.

Note: Split peas can be used instead of lentils.

Rice Pudding

Although rice pudding can be made with raw rice, the cooking time is much shorter if you begin with cooked. The pudding will be very tasty whether made from white, brown, basmati, or wild rice, and each will lend its characteristic taste to the dish. If you plan this as a breakfast dish or dessert, cook the rice in water. If you wish to serve it at a main meal, you might want to cook the rice in broth and omit the molasses and nutmeg from the pudding. Vary the seasonings as you wish—you can use maple syrup as the sweetener, or cardamom, sugar, rose water, and almonds if using basmati rice.

3 cups milk
3 eggs
½ teaspoon nutmeg
   Grated rind of 1 lemon
2 tablespoons molasses
3 cups cooked rice
½ cup raisins

Preheat oven to 350°F.

Beat the milk, eggs, nutmeg, lemon rind, and molasses together in a mixing bowl. Stir in the rice and raisins. Pour into a well-buttered baking dish and bake in preheated oven until firm, about 1 hour. Serve warm or cold.

Makes 6 to 8 servings.

Whether your memories of rice pudding (right) conjure up images of grandmother, the Automat, or the school cafeteria, you cannot be a snob about the plebeian nature of this dessert—it is simply too good.

Basic Risotto

Risotto is cooked uncovered and stirred almost constantly while hot liquid is added in stages. Serve risotto when rice is tender but before all of the broth is absorbed. It is traditionally made with Italian short-grain white Arborio rice, which has a creamy texture when cooked. It may be expensive; other short-grain converted or white rice may be substituted with reasonable results. You can use brown rice to make a risottolike dish, but it will not have the same characteristic flavor. Long-grain rice makes a risotto that is more like a pilaf.

Risotto can be seasoned with herbs, fresh vegetables, and seafood. Ingredients that cook quickly can be cut into small pieces, added to the risotto at the appropriate moment, and cooked along with the rice (additional broth may be required). Ingredients that need longer cooking or different treatments should be prepared separately and stirred in with the final addition of broth.

4½ cups homemade chicken broth, or as necessary (or use equal parts canned broth and water)

2 tablespoons butter

2 tablespoons olive oil

1 teaspoon fresh thyme, or herb(s) of choice

1 onion, peeled and finely chopped

2 cups short-grain rice, preferably Arborio

¼ cup dry white wine (optional)

¼ cup minced fresh parsley

Salt and freshly ground pepper (to taste)

¼ cup light cream (optional)

¼ cup grated Parmesan cheese

Place the broth in a small saucepan and heat to simmering. Adjust the heat as necessary and keep it simmering until the risotto is ready to serve.

Melt the butter with the olive oil in a heavy skillet or saucepan. Add the herb(s) and onion and sauté over very low heat, stirring occasionally, until tender but not brown, about 15 minutes.

Raise the heat to medium. Add the rice and cook, stirring constantly, until the grains turn transparent along the edges, about 5 minutes.

If using the wine, sprinkle over the rice and allow to evaporate. Pour enough of the broth into the pan to cover the rice, and adjust the heat so that the broth is simmering steadily. Cook, stirring constantly, until the broth is absorbed, about 5 minutes. Add broth as before and continue to cook and stir.

In this manner, continue to add broth to the rice, cooking and stirring until the grains are tender but still firm. Remove the pan from the heat. Add the parsley, salt, and pepper. Stir in the cream or enough additional broth to make a creamy sauce. Stir in the Parmesan (and additional butter if desired) and serve immediately.

Makes 4 servings.

Even a simple Risotto (left) requires constant tending, but the full flavor is more than worth the trouble.

Chilled Rice with Yogurt and Dates

This is a very easy sweet treat that is actually quite good for you. It takes only a few minutes to prepare, but it should be thoroughly chilled before serving so the flavors can blend. Serve for breakfast or dessert.

2 cups cooked rice, brown or white, as desired

½ cup chopped, pitted dates

1 apple, cored, peeled if desired, and chopped

½ cup chopped almonds

¾ cup yogurt

1 tablespoon honey (or to taste)

¼ teaspoon vanilla

Dash of nutmeg

Mix the rice with the fruit and nuts in a bowl. Mix the yogurt with the remaining ingredients, adjusting the sweetness if desired (remember that the fruit is sweet), and add to the rice mixture, stirring until everything is coated with the yogurt. Cover the bowl and refrigerate for at least 3 hours.

Makes 4 servings.

Note: Substitute a peach for the apple if the season is right.

Basmati Rice with Curry Sauce

Naturally fragrant and sweet, basmati rice is the perfect foil for a pungent curry sauce. A basic meat-free recipe follows, but you can add beef, lamb, chicken, or shrimp to the sauce if you wish. Be sure your curry powder is fresh or the results will be unexciting; if the sauce does not seem hot enough for your taste, supplement the curry powder with extra, ground cayenne pepper.

For the sauce:

2 tablespoons butter or mild-flavored oil
1 onion, peeled and chopped
2 or **3** cloves garlic, minced
2 plum tomatoes, chopped (fresh or canned)
1 small tart apple, cored and chopped
2 stalks celery, chopped
1 small green bell pepper, seeded and chopped
½ teaspoon fresh gingerroot, peeled and grated
2 tablespoons curry powder (or to taste)
3 cups broth (if using canned tomatoes, include some of their liquid)

For the rice:

1½ cups basmati rice, white or brown
3 pods whole cardamom seeds, bruised
3 cups water
½ cup slivered almonds

Heat the oil or butter in a heavy saucepan over medium heat. Add the onion and garlic and sauté until wilted, about 5 minutes. Add the tomatoes, apple, cel-ery, bell pepper, and ginger and continue to cook for 10 more minutes. Sprinkle with the curry powder, and stir to mix. Add the broth, stir, cover the pan, and simmer for 10 minutes. Taste the sauce and correct the seasonings. Puree the sauce in batches in a food processor fitted with the steel blade, or put through a food mill. Return the pureed sauce to the pan.

Meanwhile, place the rice, cardamom pods, and water in a saucepan and bring to a boil. Cover, reduce the heat, and simmer until tender, about 20 to 30 minutes. Remove the cardamom pods, and fluff the rice with a fork. If necessary, keep warm until ready to serve.

Mound the rice on a serving platter and scatter the almonds over it. Place the curry in a separate serving dish, and serve over individual portions of rice. Curry is usually accompanied by assorted condiments such as shredded coconut, chutney, dahl, and yogurt.

Makes 4 to 6 servings.

Note: You can cook a wide variety of vegetables and or meat in the pureed sauce. Cut in small pieces and add in order of their cooking times, so that none will be overcooked. (If appropriate, you can sauté them first.) Some vegetable suggestions are: cauliflower, chick-peas (cooked or canned), potatoes, green bell pepper, zucchini, green peas, spinach, onion, and carrot.

Simple Aromatic Basmati Pilaf or Poultry Stuffing

Basmati rice is naturally sweet tasting. Here it is mixed with carrots, raisins, and spices, and the long grains of the rice and the curls of the carrot are very pretty together. You can serve it as a side dish or use it to stuff a chicken.

1 cup basmati rice, white or brown
2 cups water
4 medium carrots, grated
4 to **6** tablespoons raisins (if desired)
1 teaspoon cinnamon
½ teaspoon ground cloves

Place the rice and water in a saucepan and bring to a boil. Cover, reduce the heat, and simmer until tender, about 20 to 30 minutes. If no water remains in the pan, add just enough to cover the bottom. Fluff the rice with a fork. Quickly stir in the grated carrots, raisins, and spices. Cover the pan and continue to cook without stirring until the raisins are hot, 3 to 5 minutes. If necessary, add a little more water to the pan so the rice does not stick.

Serve immediately or set aside to cool, then place loosely in the cavity of a chicken or Cornish hen.

Makes 4 servings; one-half of the recipe is enough to stuff a 3-pound chicken.

Basmati rice has a fragrant sweetness that is delightful mixed with raisins and spices, as in the Aromatic Basmati Pilaf (right).

Rye ranks next to wheat as a popular bread flour. Like many of the other grains, it probably first grew wild in southwestern Asia. It was considered a weed long before it was recognized as a valuable food crop (it is also used to make whiskey). Rye tolerates damp and cold much better than wheat, which may explain why rye bread is found so often in the cuisines of northern countries like Sweden and the Soviet Union (which grows over half the world's rye). It was brought to the New World by the Dutch and British colonists and was at one point a major crop, but today very little rye is grown in North America.

Rye has a stronger flavor than the other grains (with the exception of buckwheat), and in its whole forms is actually more nutritious than wheat (the protein in rye contains an essential amino acid that is not present in wheat), so there is considerable reason to expand the part it plays in our diet. Look for whole rye products in a health-food store; rye flour is often available at a regular grocery.

Rye is a distinctively flavored grain. It is particularly complemented by aromatic herbs such as caraway, fennel, and anise, the nutty flavors of chick-peas or chestnuts, and sweet-and-sour sauces that are based on a blend of tomato, lemon, or vinegar with honey or dried fruit. Mix it with winter vegetables such as squash, cabbage, carrots, or parsnips.

© Lynn Karlin

Rye Berries

Rye Meal

Rye Flour

Rye Berries

Whole rye berries have a nutrient-rich covering of bran. They make a hearty base for pilafs or stuffings and can be served as a side dish on their own. They are also a different and successful stir-fry ingredient. They can be cooked together with rice, added to soups, and, if precooked, to breads. They are also excellent when sprouted.

Cracked Rye or Rye Grits

Cracked rye is whole rye berries that are broken into small pieces. It is most often cooked into a porridge, but can be added to breads and muffins.

Rolled Rye or Rye Flakes

Rolled rye is the equivalent of rolled oats. The rye berries are heated until soft, and then rolled flat. Use rolled rye to make porridge or add it to granola or baked goods.

Meal

Rye meal is coarsely ground whole rye berries. It is difficult to find, but is the "flour" of choice for making delicious pumpernickel bread.

Flour

Rye flour is ground from whole rye berries. After it is ground, some of the bran that covers the berries is sifted out and the flour is graded as light, medium, or dark. The darker it is, the more of the bran and nutrients remain. The flours can be used interchangeably, but the darker the color, the more robust the final flavor will be.

Rye flour contains a limited amount of gluten and it can be used to make yeast-raised breads. However, 100-percent rye breads tend to be quite heavy, so wheat flour is often mixed with rye. Because the rye flavor is naturally strong, you can use as much as four parts wheat flour to one part rye without losing the characteristic taste. Dark rye bread is not necessarily made with dark rye flour, but may be colored with coffee, molasses, cocoa, or caramel. If you are purchasing rye bread you cannot really judge its nutritional value by its color. Read the label—the primary ingredient may be enriched wheat flour! Rye breads can be sweet-flavored or sour; they often contain cornmeal, potatoes, and/or spices. Rye flour can be used to make pancakes or muffins, but it is not usually chosen for pastry.

RYE RECIPES

Basic Steamed Rye Berries

Whole rye berries more than double in volume when they are steamed.

The exact proportion of water to grain and the length of the cooking time will vary somewhat according to size and weight of the pan, intensity of the flame, and desired degree of softness. The directions that follow are for grains that are cooked but discrete; if you wish to make a creamy porridge, increase both the amount of water and the cooking time.

Place 1 part whole rye berries and 2½ parts water in a saucepan. Bring to a boil, cover, reduce the heat, and simmer for 40 minutes.

Fluff the cooked rye with a fork and serve with butter, yogurt, or soy sauce, or use in recipes calling for cooked whole rye berries. Use this basic recipe as a guide when adding rye to soup.

Rye-plus Bread

Here is a nicely textured rye bread with more than a hint of anise. It is not a sweet bread, and if you don't have (or don't care for) anise, you can substitute caraway, onion, raisins, or fennel. This bread can be baked in rounds on a cookie sheet or in conventional loaf pans.

2	packages yeast (cake or fresh)
2	cups warm water
2	tablespoons molasses
2	cups rye flour
2	cups whole-wheat flour
2	cups all-purpose flour
1	cup cornmeal
1	tablespoon aniseed, crushed in a mortar
½	teaspoon salt
1	tablespoon unsweetened cocoa
2	tablespoons oil or melted butter
1	cup cooked rye berries (optional)

Dissolve the yeast in the warm water in a large mixing bowl. Gently stir in the molasses and let the mixture rest for about 10 minutes, until the yeast begins to bubble. In another bowl combine all the flours and dry seasonings except the rye berries and mix very thoroughly. Stir the oil or melted butter into the yeast mixture. One cup at a time, stir in most of the flour. Turn the dough onto a floured pastry board and knead until smooth and elastic, working in more flour as necessary. Shape the dough into a ball.

Oil a large bowl; place the dough in the bowl, turning it once to oil the top. Cover with a damp cloth and put in a warm place. Allow to rise until doubled in size, about 1 hour.

Punch the dough down and knead briefly on the floured board. Divide into 2 pieces and let rest while you oil and dust a cookie sheet or 2 loaf pans with cornmeal. Shape the dough into loaves and place on the sheet or in the pans. Rub a little oil on your hands and pat the tops of the loaves. Cover with a damp cloth and put in a warm place. Allow to rise until nearly doubled in size, about 30 to 40 minutes. Bake in preheated 375°F oven for 40 minutes if using the cookie sheet; 50 minutes if using loaf pans. Remove from the sheet or pans to cool.

Makes 2 loaves.

Sturdy, freshly baked loaves of Rye-plus Bread (left).

Rye Berry–Stuffed Cabbage with Chick-Peas

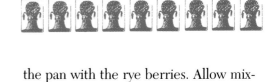

The flavors of rye berries and cabbage are particularly complementary, and the addition of chick-peas makes this a protein-rich entrée that can be made with chicken, beef, or vegetable stock as you wish. The lemon juice turns the sauce pleasantly tart. If you would like even more punch, omit the caraway and substitute coriander for the parsley.

½   cup rye berries

¼   teaspoon caraway seeds

1¼   cups water

1   small head cabbage

1   tablespoon butter

1   onion, thinly sliced

1   clove garlic, peeled and thinly sliced

1   plum tomato, seeded and chopped

¼   cup tomato juice (or liquid from plum tomato, if canned)

1   bay leaf

1   whole clove

2   cups broth, more if necessary (if using canned chicken broth, substitute 1 cup water for 1 cup broth)

¾   cup chick-peas (cooked or canned, drained)

1   clove garlic, peeled and minced

1   grated carrot

1   scallion, finely chopped

1   tablespoon minced fresh parsley

2   tablespoons yogurt

      Juice of 1 lemon

      Salt and freshly ground pepper (to taste)

1   tablespoon honey (optional)

Put the rye berries and caraway seeds in a saucepan with the water. Bring to a boil, cover, reduce the heat, and simmer for 30 minutes. Remove from the heat but do not drain the liquid. While it is cooking, prepare the cabbage and start the sauce.

To peel the leaves off the cabbage, invert it on a cutting board and, using a paring knife, remove the core to a depth of at least 1 inch. Discard any tough outer leaves that fall off. Hold the cabbage upright under cold running water and gently fold out the outermost leaf, filling it with water. Turn the cabbage as you do this. The weight of the water will release the leaf. Repeat to release 12 leaves, cutting them loose at the core as necessary. Place 10 of the leaves in a vegetable steamer, bring to a boil, and steam for 3 minutes. Remove from the steamer to cool and drain.

Melt the butter over a low heat in a Dutch oven or other large flameproof casserole. Add the onion and sliced garlic, cover, and cook, stirring occasionally, until tender and translucent, about 10 minutes. Shred the 2 unsteamed cabbage leaves and add to the onions, cooking for another 10 minutes. Add the tomato and tomato juice and continue to cook 10 minutes longer. Add the bay leaf, clove, broth, and any liquid left in the pan with the rye berries. Allow mixture to simmer, covered, while you stuff the cabbage leaves.

Combine the rye berries, chick-peas, minced garlic, carrot, scallion, and parsley in a bowl and mix well. Mix the yogurt with the juice from half the lemon and stir into the rye-berry mixture. Add salt and pepper if desired.

One at a time, place the cabbage leaves, cupping upward, on your work surface. If the stem end of the leaf is very thick, make a V-shape cut with a paring knife to remove it (try not to cut more than an inch deep into the leaf). Place a few tablespoons of the filling in the leaf, fold in the sides and then, beginning with the stem end, roll it up. Place the rolls, seam-side down, in the simmering sauce. Spoon some of the sauce over them, cover, and simmer, basting occasionally and adding more broth if necessary, for 40 minutes. Squeeze the remaining lemon juice (through a sieve) over the cabbage rolls and cook 10 minutes longer.

Spoon the cabbage rolls onto a serving platter or into individual bowls and keep warm. Remove the bay leaf and whole clove from the sauce. Taste and add honey if desired. Spoon the sauce over the rolls and serve at once.

Makes 4 to 5 servings.

Borscht with Rye Berries

For this hearty classic, you can chop and add the vegetables as you work down the ingredients list. Chop the ingredients finely as indicated (use your food processor for everything except the tomatoes, if you like) so that they cook fairly quickly. Once cooked, the soup should sit for several hours to completely blend the flavors, so plan to adjust the sweet/sour seasonings before you serve it.

1   cup rye berries
2½ cups water
2   tablespoons butter or oil
1   large onion, finely chopped
1   carrot, finely chopped
1   green bell pepper, cored, seeded, and finely chopped
1   small head green cabbage, coarsely shredded
1   beet, peeled and finely chopped
1   stalk celery, diced
1   small tart apple, cored and diced
1   boiling potato, peeled and chopped
2   cups canned tomatoes, drained and chopped
4   cloves garlic, peeled and minced
2   quarts water or stock
    Bouquet garni: 1 bay leaf, 5 peppercorns, 3 juniper berries, ¼ teaspoon caraway seeds, and 3 sprigs parsley, all tied in a piece of cheesecloth
    Salt and freshly ground pepper (to taste)
½   teaspoon honey (or to taste)
    Juice of 1 lemon (or to taste)
    Garnishes: yogurt or sour cream, minced fresh parsley

Place the rye berries and water in a saucepan, bring to a boil, cover, reduce the heat, and let simmer while you prepare the rest of the soup.

In a large stockpot, melt the butter or oil. Add the vegetables in the order listed, sautéeing each for about 2 minutes before adding the next. Add the stock, bouquet garni, and the rye berries with their cooking liquid. Bring to a boil, reduce the heat, cover the pot, and simmer for 20 minutes or until everything is tender. Add the salt, pepper, honey, and lemon juice in small batches, tasting as you go.

Remove the soup from the heat and let stand for 2 to 3 hours or refrigerate overnight. Remove the bouquet garni, reheat, adjust the seasonings and serve garnished with a dollop of yogurt or sour cream and parsley.

Makes ten to twelve 1-cup servings.

Rye Buttermilk Pancakes with Poppy Seeds

This is a nicely flavored variation on an old-fashioned theme. Try serving the pancakes with a hot syrup made of equal parts of honey and orange juice.

1   teaspoon poppy seeds
1   teaspoon sugar
½   teaspoon grated fresh lemon rind
1   teaspoon hot water
1   cup rye flour
½   teaspoon baking soda
½   teaspoon salt
1   cup buttermilk
1   tablespoon melted butter
1   egg, lightly beaten

Mix the poppy seeds with the sugar, lemon rind, and hot water. Sift the dry ingredients together into a mixing bowl and make a well in the center. Blend the buttermilk, butter, and egg together with the poppy seed mixture and add to the flour, whisking together with just a few strokes (don't try to eliminate all the lumps). Cover the bowl and let stand for at least 1 hour or refrigerate overnight.

Heat a griddle to medium-low. Spoon or pour on the batter until it spreads to the desired size. Cook the pancakes until bubbles rise to the surface and just begin to break; flip and continue to cook till the other side is done. Pancakes can be kept on a plate in a warm oven until ready to serve.

Makes six 6-inch pancakes.

Rye Borscht (left) is a feast for palate and eye.

Despite its exotic sounding name (*trit-i-kay-lee*), this is one grain that cannot claim to have nourished an ancient civilization. A cross between wheat—scientifically known as *triticum*—and rye—*secale*—triticale was first developed in the late nineteenth century in an effort to combine the best qualities of each, and perhaps solve the world's hunger problems. Scientists were not able to overcome the hybrid's sterility until the 1930s. Eventually varieties of triticale were developed that have the climatic tolerance and nutritional advantages of rye mixed with the high yield and baking qualities of wheat—and taste good as well. Triticale is not yet the wonder grain of the future, and, unfortunately, most people are completely unfamiliar with it. Look for it at health-food stores, where you may find it in pasta, snacks, and cereals, as well as in various forms of refinement.

Not surprisingly, triticale tastes like both wheat and rye. With a little experimentation, it can be substituted for either. The berries have a nutty flavor and are excellent in pilafs and salads. They are very versatile and can be seasoned in numerous ways. Complement triticale as you would rice, but bear in mind that its flavor is strong enough to overpower a very delicate sauce.

WHAT TO LOOK FOR IN THE MARKET

Berries

Triticale berries have a flavor that is similar to wild rice and can be used much as wheat or rye berries or rice are—cooked whole for porridge or a side dish, or added to soups, casseroles, and baked goods. Cook triticale together with wild or regular rice for a simple but different side dish.

Flakes

Triticale flakes are similar to rolled oats, rye, or wheat. They can be cooked into porridge, toasted for dry cereal, or added to breads, muffins, and cookies.

Triticale Flour

Flour

Triticale flour is ground from whole triticale berries. It contains more gluten than rye flour, for which it can be substituted in any recipe, but this gluten is very delicate and must be handled gently. With care, triticale flour can be used as the sole or primary flour in yeast-raised bread. Knead it as little as possible, just to work in the flour, and let it rise only once (place the dough in loaf pans right after the first kneading and bake directly after it is risen). If it is overhandled, the gluten will be destroyed and the results will be unappetizingly heavy. If desired, triticale flour can be substituted successfully for wheat flour in all sorts of nonyeast recipes (try it in pancakes or crust for vegetable pie); it will lend a pleasant wheaty-rye flavor.

TRITICALE RECIPES

Basic Steamed Triticale Berries

Whole triticale berries double in volume when they are steamed.
The exact proportion of water to grain and the length of the cooking time will vary somewhat in each individual kitchen—the size and weight of the pan, the intensity of the flame, and the desired degree of softness all influence the results. The directions that follow are for grains that are cooked but discrete; if you wish to make a creamy porridge, increase both the amount of water and the cooking time.

Place 1 part whole triticale berries and 1½ parts water in a saucepan. Bring to a boil, cover, reduce the heat, and simmer for 50 minutes. If there is water remaining in the pan when the berries are done, drain it; it can be saved for soup stock.

Fluff the cooked triticale with a fork and serve with butter, yogurt, or soy sauce, or use in recipes calling for cooked whole triticale. You can use this basic recipe as a guide when adding triticale to soup.

Triticale and Black Beans

Combine triticale with meaty black beans and a zesty dash of cumin, and serve as a hearty main or side dish. The beans take about an hour and half to cook, the triticale 50 minutes, so pace yourself accordingly.

1	*cup black beans, soaked overnight and drained*
5½	*cups water*
1	*cup triticale berries*
3	*tablespoons olive oil*
1	*onion, peeled and diced*
3	*or* **4** *cloves garlic, peeled and finely chopped*
1	*green bell pepper, cored, seeded, and diced*
¾	*teaspoon cumin seed, crushed or ground*
2	*teaspoons minced fresh oregano*
	Salt and freshly ground pepper (to taste)

Combine the beans and 4 cups of the water in a saucepan. Bring to a boil, cover, reduce the heat, and simmer until tender, about 1½ hours. After 40 minutes, start to cook the triticale in the remaining water (see above). Drain the beans when done.

Heat the olive oil in a skillet over medium heat and sauté the onion, garlic, and bell pepper until the onion wilts, 4 to 5 minutes. Stir in the cumin seed and oregano. Stir in the beans and mix well. Toss the bean mixture with the cooked triticale in a serving dish and season with salt and pepper.

Makes 4 servings.

© Bill Milne

Triticale and Black Beans (left).

Triticale Bread

Triticale bread is tricky to make, but if you are curious about its wheaty-rye flavor you may want to try this recipe.

1   package yeast (cake or fresh)
2   cups warm water
1   tablespoon molasses
2   tablespoons butter or oil
½   teaspoon salt
2½ cups all-purpose flour
2½ cups triticale flour

In a small bowl, dissolve the yeast in the warm water and set aside until it begins to bubble, about 5 minutes. Add the molasses and butter or oil.

Add the salt and all-purpose flour and stir the batter for about 5 minutes to develop the gluten. Add the triticale flour, working as quickly and gently as possible. Turn the mixture onto a pastry board to knead in any flour that is not readily stirred in. Divide the dough into 2 pieces; let them rest while you oil 2 loaf pans. Shape the dough into loaves and put into the pans. Put some oil on your hands and pat the tops of the loaves to oil them. Cover with a damp cloth and put in a warm place. Let rise until doubled in size, 1 to 1½ hours.

Meanwhile, preheat the oven to 350°F. When the loaves have risen, put them in the oven and bake until done, about 1 hour.

Makes 2 loaves.

Triticale Pilaf with Watercress and Pecans

A very fresh pilaf that is a perfect accompaniment to lightly seasoned poultry or seafood. You can serve this hot, cold or at room temperature, as you wish, but be sure to mix it hot so that the flavors blend and the watercress wilts just a bit.

1½ cups triticale berries
2¼ cups water
¾   cup pecan meats, broken
1   cup scallions, chopped
    Grated rind of 1 lemon
1   bunch watercress, washed, dried, and cut into small sprigs
4   tablespoons olive oil
1   tablespoon vinegar (preferably rosemary or other herbal flavor)
    Salt and freshly ground pepper (to taste)

Preheat oven to 375°F.

Cook the triticale berries in the water, following the basic directions on page 79. While they are steaming, toast the pecan meats (on a small cookie sheet) in preheated oven for about 15 minutes, or until they begin to darken. Set aside.

When the triticale is done, drain any excess water from the pan and return it to a very low heat. Quickly stir in the pecans, scallions, lemon rind, watercress, oil, and vinegar. Adjust the seasonings, adding salt and pepper, and remove from the heat.

Makes 4 to 6 servings.

Triticale Poultry Stuffing with Lentils and Apples

A bird stuffed with this hearty mix really requires no other accompaniment, except perhaps a fresh salad. If not all of the stuffing fits in the chest cavity, place it in a covered casserole with a little chicken or vegetable broth and heat in the oven for the last 20 minutes of the roasting time. (If you happen to have leftover chicken or turkey, you can mix it in with this pilaf and heat it all together for a quick one-dish meal.)

1   cup cooked triticale berries
1   cup cooked lentils
1   tart apple, cored and cut into small chunks
¼   cup almonds, sliced or coarsely chopped
1   or 2 shallots, peeled and diced
    Grated rind of 1 lemon
    Salt and freshly ground pepper (to taste)

Mix all the ingredients together in a bowl, then stuff loosely into the cavity of a bird.

Makes approximately 3 cups, enough for a 4-pound chicken; halve or double as desired.

The ingredients for Triticale Poultry Stuffing with Lentils and Apples (right) ready to go into bird or casserole.

WHEAT

© Visual Horizons/FPG International

The "amber waves" of wheat fields that fill the prairies of many nations mark the world's largest food crop. Wheat is probably the most commonly eaten grain in Western cultures. Because of its wonderful ability to rise and its smooth whiteness when refined, it is considered by many to be an aristocrat among grains.

Wheat may be descended from a wild grass that grew in southwestern Asia thousands of years ago, or it may have originated in the Middle East. It has been cultivated since at least 4000 B.C. It was probably the Egyptians who discovered that yeast caused wheat flour mixed with liquid to rise.

Wheat is available in more forms than any other grain, from sweet whole berries to the finest pastry flour. Except for the inedible hull that protects the kernels while they grow, each of its parts has a culinary use of its own. The array of beautiful and delicious baked goods that can be created from wheat flour has no equal among the other grains. Unfortunately, the cachet associated with highly refined wheat products has more to do with the perceived sophistication of their uses (and, you have to admit, the resulting tastiness) than with their nutritive value.

Wheat is good for you. It contains protein, vitamins, minerals, and fiber. As with the other grains, most of these nutrients are in the bran that covers the berry or in the germ that produces a new plant. Wheat is available in many "whole" forms—berries, cracked, and flour—and whole-wheat products have a pronounced flavor and a robust (to some, heavy) texture. The more wheat is refined (separated from the bran and germ), the whiter its color, the fainter its flavor, the lighter its texture, the more varied its uses, and sadly, the lower its value as food. However, unless you have an extremely rigorous attitude toward eating nutritiously, you will no doubt find that all forms of wheat have an appropriate place in your diet.

VARIETIES

There are many varieties of wheat grown around the world, and it is useful to understand something about the terms applied to them. Wheat falls into two basic crop types: *winter* and *spring*. Winter wheat, grown in mild climates, is planted in the fall and harvested the following summer; its kernel is high in starch. Spring wheat, grown in cooler climates, is planted in the spring and harvested in the fall; it is higher in protein than the winter variety. To make things more confusing, there are two subcategories in each of these seasonal types—*hard* and *soft*. It is these terms, which indicate different culinary characteristics, that really concern the cook.

Hard wheat is higher in protein than soft wheat and therefore contains more gluten. As a result, it is most often milled into bread flour. *Durum wheat* is a hard spring wheat that is used to make pasta; some people consider it the only proper wheat for that purpose.

Soft wheat contains less protein (and therefore less gluten) than hard wheat. It is usually milled into pastry flour, which is not used with yeast and so does not rely as much upon the wheat's gluten content to rise.

When you shop for wheat you do not usually need to be concerned about whether it is winter or spring, hard or soft. Indeed, you will rarely find this distinction indicated on a package label. However, occasionally you will come across a recipe that calls for soft rather than hard wheat berries, and durum wheat, or its refined form, *semolina*, is indicated as an ingredient when it has been used. For more information on flour, see page 84.

WHAT TO LOOK FOR IN THE MARKET

Whole Wheat Berries

Cracked Wheat

Whole Wheat Berries
Whole wheat berries are wheat seeds with only the inedible hull removed. They can be served on their own as porridge or a side dish and added to soups or, if precooked, to baked goods. You can use wheat berries as you would rice, but many prefer the taste or texture of either cracked wheat or bulgur (see below) for some dishes. When sprouted, whole wheat berries are very sweet and give a nice taste and texture to breads, salads, or casseroles.

Cracked Wheat
Cracked wheat is whole wheat berries that have been cut into coarse pieces with steel blades, much like steel-cut oats. It has not been refined or precooked. Cracked wheat cooks more quickly than whole wheat berries, and can be used on its own or incorporated into other dishes.

Bulgur Wheat

Bulgur

Bulgur is the wheat equivalent of kasha. It is made from wheat berries that are parboiled, dried, and then broken into pieces. It may or may not be *whole* wheat, so check the label. Bulgur is available in three grades: coarse, medium, and fine. Like kasha, bulgur is very quick cooking; it can be reconstituted by soaking in liquid.

Wheat in a few of its many manifestations (opposite page).

Couscous

The term couscous—tiny pellets that are steamed over a stew to make the North African dish of the same name—may be applied to several products, depending upon who is packaging it. In the United States it is most often a form of pasta, but it is more traditionally made from parboiled and finely cracked wheat or millet. The package will tell you which type it is.

Rolled or Flakes

Like other rolled grains, wheat flakes are made by steaming the berries until soft and then flattening with rollers. They may or may not be made from *whole* wheat. Wheat flakes can be used like rolled oats: quickly cooked into porridge, toasted for dry cereal, or added to breads, muffins, and cookies.

Flour

As mentioned, wheat flour is very high in gluten and has wonderful baking qualities. It is ground from whole wheat berries. Frequently the bran and germ are sifted out to make the flour white. For thousands of years white flour was considered more desirable than whole wheat flour (which used to be called entire wheat flour), both because it made more delicate breads and pastries and because, lacking the germ, it kept better.

The bran and germ were originally separated (bolted) from the white endosperm by sifting the ground wheat through a fine cloth. This was a very laborious process, so white flour was a luxury. It was not until the mid-nineteenth century that a steam-roller milling process was developed to separate the flour inexpensively.

Wheat Flour

Wheat flour is available in two basic degrees of refinement—whole wheat and white—each of which may be available in more than one form. Incidentally, the ability of flour to absorb liquid is affected by the type of wheat from which it is milled and the amount of bran that it contains. That is why recipes, particularly for bread, do not always specify an exact amount of flour.

Whole wheat flour is simply ground whole wheat berries. It contains the bran and germ as well as the endosperm and has a hearty taste and medium-brown color. It has a greater nutrient value than its white counterpart.

Graham is a rather flexible term that is often applied to whole wheat flour; its meaning seems to change with the miller. Sylvester Graham was a nineteenth-century American dietary reformer who, influenced by the Shakers, felt that to mill white flour was to undo God's work. Some brands of graham flour are described as being particularly coarse, some as having some of the bran removed, some as having the bran coarsely ground while the endosperm is more finely ground. Some cookbooks use the

terms whole wheat flour and graham flour interchangeably, and some indicate that there is a distinction. If you wish to use graham flour, plan to experiment, as each brand may perform a little differently. Whole wheat and graham flours should always be used quickly, and should be refrigerated or frozen so that the oils in the germ do not spoil and turn them rancid.

White flour is wheat flour from which the bran and germ have been removed, and therefore lacks much of the nutrient value found in whole wheat. Because of this, it is frequently *enriched* before it is sold—some, but not nearly all, of the vitamins and minerals that were milled away are replaced. Sometimes white flour is further refined by *bleaching*, which further destroys the nutrients. *Semolina* is white flour that is refined from durum wheat; it is used to make pasta. White flour has a long shelf life; it can be refrigerated or frozen if you choose to do so.

The Terms Used to Describe Flour: What Do They Mean?

All-purpose flour is a blend of hard and soft wheat flours. It is the type of flour you most commonly see at the grocery. It can be used for most everyday baking needs. Sometimes it is **presifted.** If you are particularly concerned about the lightness of your baked goods, sift it again before measuring. You may find that different brands perform somewhat differently, but they are basically interchangeable.

Stone-ground Flour

Gluten Flour

Stone-ground flour is not subjected to as much heat as flour that is ground with metal rollers, so it retains more of its nutrients. You may feel that it has more flavor as well.

Pastry and *cake* flours are ground from soft wheat. As their names imply, they are used for light-textured desserts. You can usually find whole wheat pastry flour at a health-food store, but it will have a stronger taste than the white varieties. If you must substitute all-purpose flour for pastry flour, use a little bit less.

Gluten flour is wheat flour supplemented with protein to increase its ability to rise. It is primarily used by commercial bakers, but is available at some specialty stores. If you mix it with low- or non-gluten flours when baking bread, you may get a lighter loaf.

Wheat Germ

The smallest part of the wheat berry is the germ, which, like the bran, contains a high proportion of the grain's nutrients. It is the only part of the wheat berry to contain vitamin E. Wheat germ, like the germ of any grain, contains oils that can spoil very quickly. Raw wheat germ should always be refrigerated. Toasted wheat germ packed in an airtight container has a reasonably long shelf life, but once it has been opened it should be refrigerated. Toasting enhances the flavor of wheat germ, but it also eliminates some of its nutritive value, so it is sometimes sold enriched. Wheat germ can add flavor and crunch to just about anything—use it to top desserts or yogurt, mix it into cereals, breads, casseroles, or side dishes.

WHEAT RECIPES

How to Cook Cracked Wheat and Bulgur

Cracked wheat and bulgur double in size when steamed.

They can be cooked following the directions for cooking whole wheat berries (allow 2½ parts liquid to 1 part grain), but bear in mind that the cooking time will vary depending upon the degree of coarseness of the grind. In general, cracked wheat will cook in about 30 minutes; bulgur (which is parboiled before it is cracked) will cook in about 15 minutes. Bulgur is often cooked in broth if it is to be used as pilaf. It can be sautéed in butter or oil before the liquid is added. Bulgur can also be reconstituted simply by soaking, but more time must be allowed for the grains to soften.

Basic Steamed Wheat Berries

Whole wheat berries double in volume when steamed.

The exact proportion of water to grain and the length of the cooking time will vary somewhat in each individual kitchen—the size and weight of the pan, the intensity of the flame, and the desired degree of softness all influence the results. The directions that follow are for grains that are cooked but discrete; if you wish to make a creamy porridge, increase both the amount of water and the cooking time.

Place 1 part whole wheat berries and 2½ parts water in a saucepan. Bring to a boil, cover, reduce the heat, and simmer for 40 minutes.

Fluff the cooked wheat berries with a fork and serve with butter, yogurt, or soy sauce, or use in recipes calling for cooked whole wheat berries. You can use this basic recipe as a guide when adding wheat berries to soup.

Basic Steamed Wheat Berries can be tossed with a few chopped apricots, scallions, and almonds to make an instant pilaf (left).

Basic White Bread

You can make this recipe using water or milk as the liquid. If you use water, the loaves will be light but firm enough to slice; with milk, they will be richer and denser (and slower to rise). If you find plain white bread unexciting, you will appreciate this as a versatile basic—with a little imagination you can change the character of the loaves. (Some variations follow the recipe.) This dough is firm enough to bake in rounds on a cookie sheet.

1   *package yeast (cake or fresh)*

2   *cups lukewarm water or milk (scalded and cooled to lukewarm)*

2   *teaspoons sugar*

2   *tablespoons mild-flavored oil or melted butter*

5½ to **6** *cups all-purpose flour (or blend with up to 4 cups whole wheat flour)*

1   *teaspoon salt*

In a large mixing bowl, dissolve yeast in warm liquid. Gently stir in sugar and let mixture rest for about 10 minutes, until yeast begins to bubble. Stir oil or butter into yeast mixture. In a measuring cup combine 2 cups of the flour with the salt. One cup at a time, stir it and 3 more cups of flour into the yeast mixture. Turn the dough onto a floured pastry board and knead until smooth and elastic, working in more flour as necessary. Shape dough into a ball.

Oil a large bowl; place the dough in the bowl, turning it once to oil the top. Cover with a damp cloth and put in a warm place. Allow to rise until doubled in size, 1 to 1½ hours.

Punch the dough down and knead it briefly on the floured board. Divide into 2 pieces and let rest while you oil a cookie sheet or 2 loaf pans. Shape the dough into loaves and place on the sheet or in the pans. Rub a little oil on your hands and pat the tops of the loaves. Cover with a damp cloth and put in a warm place. Allow to rise until nearly doubled in size, about 30 to 40 minutes.

Bake in preheated oven at 375°F for 40 minutes if using the cookie sheet, 50 minutes if using loaf pans. Remove from the sheet or pans to cool.

Makes 2 loaves.

Variations:

Poppy-Seed Bread: Soak 3 tablespoons poppy seeds and the grated rind of 1 lemon in 2 tablespoons hot water; knead into the dough after the first rising.

Raisin Bread: Add 2 tablespoons sugar to the yeast and liquid and add 1 teaspoon cinnamon or nutmeg with the salt and flour if desired; knead in 1 cup of raisins after the first rising.

Cinnamon Bread: Melt 4 tablespoons butter and cool slightly. When ready to shape loaves, flatten into rectangles, spread with melted butter and sprinkle with brown sugar and cinnamon, then roll up jelly roll–style. (You can do this in combination with the raisin bread described above if you like.)

Onion Bread: Sauté a chopped onion in butter or oil until golden and soft (or crispy if you prefer). When ready to shape loaves, flatten the dough into rectangles, spread with the onion, then roll up jelly roll–style.

Basic White Bread (right) is a classic, and a good first recipe for the novice baker—refer to the Appendix for detailed bread-baking directions.

Pizzette

Here is a light variation on the classic, heavy pizza. There are endless possibilities for pizzette toppings. Three are suggested below, but your culinary imagination may tempt you to create others. The leek topping is hearty enough to serve as a main course, the potato or salade versions are terrific appetizers or side dishes. In truth, how you incorporate pizzette into your menu really depends upon how much of it you like to eat!

The dough (crisp and airy when baked) is simple to prepare and should be started about 2 hours before you put it in the oven. If you prefer, it can be mixed ahead, allowed to rise, punched down, and refrigerated—just let it reach room temperature before you shape it for the pan.

For the dough (all ingredients should be at room temperature):

⅔	*cup white flour*
⅔	*cup whole wheat flour*
¼	*teaspoon salt*
2	*teaspoons dried or 1 teaspoon fresh herbes de Provence*
½	*package yeast (cake or fresh)*
⅓	*cup very warm water*
1	*egg*
	Olive oil to lubricate bowl

Mix all of the dry ingredients together in a warm mixing bowl and make a well in the center. Sprinkle (or crumble) the yeast into the well, gently pour in the warm water, and let stand for about 5 minutes, until the yeast begins to bubble. Break the egg into the yeast-water

mixture and beat together very gently with a fork or whisk. Gradually draw in flour from the edges of the bowl; use your fingers to mix as the dough begins to get sticky. When enough of the flour is mixed with the liquid to make a soft dough, turn the contents of the bowl onto a pastry board and knead until smooth and elastic (about 5 minutes), working in more flour as necessary.

Lightly coat the interior of a large bowl with olive oil. Shape the dough into a ball, put it in the bowl, and turn once to coat with oil. Cover the bowl with a damp cloth and set in a warm place for about 1 hour, until the dough is doubled in size.

While the dough is rising, prepare one or more of the toppings described on page 92 and at right.

When the dough has doubled in size, punch it down and turn it onto a lightly floured pastry board. Shape it into one or more flattish balls (depending on the size of the pizza pans you plan to use) and allow it to rest for a few minutes. Press each ball of dough into a pan, working it out from the center toward the edge with the heel of your hand. If you are using a shallow baking pan rather than a flat pizza pan, work the dough partway up the sides. It should be quite thin.

Arrange the topping of your choice over the dough as explained below. Turn the oven on to 375°F. Set the pizzette in a warm place to rise while the oven is heating, about 15 minutes. Bake for 20 to 25 minutes; serve immediately.

Makes one 14-inch pie.

Leek Topping

To suit your palate, any one of the following ingredients, except the leeks and oil, may be omitted altogether or replaced with a reasonable substitute.

1	*tablespoon olive oil*
3	*to 4 good-size leeks, white parts only, clean and thinly sliced*
	Freshly ground black pepper
	Pinch of fresh thyme
¼	*cup sun-dried tomatoes, coarsely chopped*
½	*can anchovy fillets*
2	*ounces goat cheese (a somewhat crumbly variety, such as Montrachet or Boucheron)*
2	*tablespoons Niçoise olives*

Heat the oil in a heavy frying pan over low heat. Add the leeks and stir to coat. Press a piece of aluminum foil directly on top of the leeks; place a cover on the pan if you have one. Cook for about 25 minutes, stirring occasionally. Stir in the pepper and thyme, and remove the pan from the heat.

Let the leeks cool slightly, then spread them over the pizzette dough in the pan. Sprinkle with the sun-dried tomatoes. Arrange the anchovies over the leeks and tomatoes so that they radiate out from the center of the pan. Crumble the cheese in between the anchovies. Scatter the olives over all. (Be sure to let your guest know that there are pits in the olives!) Set aside to rise and bake as instructed above.

Individual Pizettes, shown at left with Salade Topping (page 92).

Rosemary–New Potato Topping

It may seem odd to add potatoes to pizzette dough, but this is a very tasty treat and not nearly as heavy as a potato knish or pancake!

2   or **3** *new potatoes, very thinly sliced*
1   *clove garlic, peeled and minced (or more to taste)*
1   *teaspoon fresh rosemary leaves, coarsely chopped*
     Olive oil
     Grated Parmesan cheese or salt (if desired)
     Freshly ground pepper (to taste)

Combine the sliced potatoes, garlic, and rosemary in a small bowl and toss with just enough olive oil to coat. Lightly brush the pizzette dough with a little olive oil. Arrange the potatoes, one slice deep, in an attractive pattern on the dough, sprinkle with a little Parmesan or salt and the pepper, and bake as instructed above.

Salade Topping

This is a surprising way to serve salad, but the wilted leaves are actually very good warmed. If you like, you can toss a little Parmesan cheese in with the oil.

     Approximately 2 cups assorted salad leaves: watercress, radicchio, endive, escarole frisé, washed, dried, and coarsely chopped
     Freshly ground pepper
     Olive oil
1   *clove garlic, peeled and minced (if desired)*

In a bowl, toss the salad leaves with the pepper and just enough olive oil to coat. Brush a little oil on the dough and sprinkle with the minced garlic, and bake as instructed above. Spread the salad leaves over the pizzette when 5 minutes of baking time remain.

Light and Tasty Wheat Bread with Herbs

Here is a bread with a crisp crust that hides a remarkably light loaf. It is a perfect choice to serve warm with a meal, but is too fragile for sandwiches. The dough rises beautifully when placed in either loaf pans or 7-inch casseroles; try baking it in muffin tins for dinner rolls. The herbs, of course, are optional, but they do add a wonderful flavor.

3   *cups whole wheat flour*
2   *cups all-purpose flour*
¾   *teaspoon salt*
1   *package yeast (cake or fresh)*
2   *cups warm water*
1   *tablespoon honey*
2   *tablespoons olive oil*
1   *teaspoon herbes de Provence*

Place the flours and salt in a large mixing bowl. Mix together and make a deep well in the center. Place the yeast in the well, pour a ½ cup of the water over it,

add the honey, oil, and herbes de Provence, and stir gently. Stir in a bit of the flour and let mixture rest for about 10 minutes until yeast begins to bubble. Slowly add remaining water and gradually stir in the rest of the flour to make a soft, slightly sticky dough.

Dust a pastry board with flour. Turn the dough onto the board and knead until smooth and elastic. Oil a large bowl; place the dough in the bowl, turning it once to oil the top. Cover with a damp cloth and put in a warm place. Allow to rise until doubled in size, about 1 hour.

Punch the dough down and return to the floured board. Divide in half, shape into loaves, and place in oiled baking pans. Cover and let rise until doubled in size, about 30 minutes.

Preheat the oven to 375°F. Bake for 50 to 60 minutes. Remove from the pans to cool on wire racks.

Makes 2 loaves.

Wheat Berry White Bean Soup

The flavor of this soup is surprisingly delicate. Serve it with herbed wheat bread and a salad tossed with Parmesan (double the recipe to serve as a main course). If fresh basil is not available, add some dried basil to the soup and use parsley for the garnish.

It is a snap to make, but both the wheat berries and the beans must be soaked overnight and then everything must simmer long enough to blend the flavors. If you wish to shorten the preparation time, you can cook the beans ahead, draining them and reserving a ½ cup of the cooking liquid. Refrigerate until you are ready to make the soup.

For the soup:
1   *cup white beans (Great Northern or smaller), soaked overnight and drained*
        Water
2   *tablespoons olive oil*
1   *onion, coarsely chopped*
1   *carrot, peeled and coarsely chopped*
1   *stalk celery, coarsely chopped*
3   *cloves garlic, peeled and minced*
        Pinch of thyme
2   *plum tomatoes (canned are fine)*
3½ *cups water*
1   *cup wheat berries, soaked overnight and drained*
1   *tablespoon chopped fresh basil*
        Salt and freshly ground pepper (to taste)

For the garnish (you can adjust the proportions to taste):
¼   *cup fresh basil leaves, rinsed and dried*
1   *clove garlic, peeled*
4   *tablespoons olive oil*

Place the beans in a saucepan, cover with 2 inches of water and bring to a boil. Reduce the heat, cover the pan, and simmer for about 1½ hours, until the beans are tender. (Check the beans occasionally, adding more water if necessary.) Drain the beans.

Heat oil in a heavy saucepan over medium heat and sauté onion, carrot, celery, garlic, and thyme for about 8 minutes, stirring frequently. Crush plum tomatoes with a spoon and add to the pan. Stir to mix and continue to sauté for a moment. Add water, stir, bring to a boil, cover, and reduce heat. Simmer vegetables for about 30 minutes.

Puree the vegetables with their broth in a food processor fitted with the metal blade. Return to the pan. Put the cooked beans with ½ cup of their cooking liquid in the food processor and pulse twice. Add to the vegetables and stir well. Cover the pan and cook over medium heat until the mixture begins to simmer. Stir the wheat berries into the vegetables. Continue to simmer the soup over low heat for about 45 minutes, stirring frequently so that it doesn't stick to the bottom of the pan; add more water if the mixture becomes too thick. When the wheat berries are tender, stir in 1 tablespoon of chopped basil, salt, and pepper.

For the garnish, chop the basil leaves with a clove of garlic in the food processor or a wooden bowl. Blend with the olive oil.

Serve the soup with a spoonful of the garnish in each bowl.

Makes 6 servings.

Basic Pie Crust

The only secret to a successful pie crust is to have the ingredients very cold and to put them together as quickly as possible. You can mix pie crust directly on a pastry board or in a mixing bowl, as you prefer. The dough can be frozen if you do not need to use it all at once.

This crust can be used for nearly any pie, whether custard, fruit, or meat. A rule for easy fruit pie follows the recipe.

1½   *cups all-purpose flour*
1   *teaspoon baking powder*
¼   *teaspoon salt*
    Dash of nutmeg (optional)
8   *tablespoons butter, chilled*
5   *to* 6 *tablespoons ice water*

Sift the dry ingredients together. Cut in the butter with a pastry blender; it should be pea-size. Sprinkle 5 tablespoons of the water over the flour mixture; combine quickly with a fork. Gather the dough together with your fingers. If it is too dry to hold together, mix in another tablespoon of water. Knead the dough once or twice to finish mixing. Divide in 2 pieces and wrap each in wax paper or plastic wrap. Refrigerate for at least 1 hour.

Dust a pastry board and a rolling pin with flour. Roll out a piece of the dough until it is somewhat bigger than your pie pan. (If the dough sticks, gently lift the dough and redust the board, and keep your rolling pin dusted.) Dust the top of the dough very lightly with flour, fold it loosely in quarters, and transfer to the pie pan. Press it gently into shape. To join or patch any tears or scallops along the edge, moisten the dough very lightly with water and press the layers together.

Fill the pie shell as desired. Roll out the second piece of dough as before and place over the filled shell, if desired. Using a sharp knife and rotating the pie pan, trim the dough evenly about ½ inch beyond the edge of the pan. Fold the 2 layers of dough under together and crimp or flute as desired. Pierce the top crust with a fork or knife and brush with beaten egg if desired. Bake in a 375°F oven for 45 minutes to 1 hour, or until filling is done and crust is golden brown. If the crust browns too quickly along the edges, cover with strips of foil.

Note: You can substitute ½ cup ground nuts for ½ cup of the flour. If you do, use only 6 to 7 tablespoons of butter.

Rule for Easy Fruit Pie

Before you put the crust into your pie pan, peel and slice the fruit and put it in the pan to be sure you have enough. If you are making a pie with a top crust, you can mound in the fruit; if you are making an open tart, fill the pan neatly. Transfer the fruit to a mixing bowl and wipe out the pie pan. Sprinkle sugar over the fruit (fresh fruit rarely need more than 2 to 3 tablespoons of sugar) drizzle with honey, or beat an egg with any seasonings desired (suggestions follow) and mix it with the fruit and sugar.

For a special touch, add cinnamon and nutmeg or crumbled blue cheese to apples or pears, cardamom or hyssop to peaches, grated lemon rind to blueberries or raspberries, or almond extract to cherries. You can also add a tablespoon of brandy or another liqueur.

At right, Basic Pie Crust, filled with apples, following the Rule for Easy Fruit Pie.

Classic Tabbouleh

Tabbouleh is a bulgur-based Middle-Eastern salad that is traditionally flavored with parsley and fresh mint. In this version, all the ingredients are layered in a casserole and refrigerated for at least 24 hours until the flavors are subtly blended. Toss the ingredients together when you are ready to serve the salad. If you remove only the portion you plan to eat and keep the remainder in the covered casserole, layers undisturbed, it will last for several days.

To make a good tabbouleh you must have ripe tomatoes, so summer is really the best time to eat it. It makes a delightful vegetarian main course in hot weather. Serve it on a bed of lettuce, sprinkled with feta cheese and accompanied by hummus and pita bread. (If you are feeling all-American, fresh, hot corn on the cob is another complementary accompaniment.)

Classic Tabbouleh, garnished with feta cheese and served with pita bread (left), is a mixture of bulgur soaked in lemon juice and olive oil, and fresh summer vegetables.

1	*cup bulgur, coarse or medium grind*
½	*cup olive oil*
	Juice of 4 large lemons (at least ¾ cup)
1	*cup scallions, finely chopped (include the green part)*
2	*cups fresh parsley, finely chopped and mixed with ½ cup fresh mint, finely chopped*
2	*cups juicy ripe tomatoes, cored and finely chopped*
¾	*cup cucumber, finely chopped (use small firm ones)*

Spread the bulgur in the bottom of a 10-inch-square casserole that has a tight-fitting lid. Whisk the olive oil together with the lemon juice until blended and pour over the bulgur. Beginning with the scallions, add the chopped vegetables in the order listed, spreading each in an even layer over the preceding one. Cover the casserole and refrigerate for 24 hours or longer before serving.

Makes 4 main-course servings; 8 side-dish servings. If you halve or double the recipe, adjust the size of the casserole so the proportion of the layers does not change greatly.

Note: Everything except the tomatoes can be chopped in a food processor. The proportions of the vegetables can be varied to taste.

Lemon-Parsley Bulgur Pilaf with Chestnuts and Brussels Sprouts

Here is a subtly lemon-flavored winter pilaf that is a good accompaniment to a simple roast chicken. If you like brussels sprouts, you'll savor the flavors of this dish; if you don't care for them, leave them out. In fact, if you triple the number of chestnuts and eliminate the sprouts, you will have a rather sophisticated side dish.

8	*chestnuts*
1	*package fresh brussels sprouts (about 2 dozen)*
3	*tablespoons olive oil*
1	*small onion, finely chopped*
⅔	*cup coarse bulgur*
	Juice of half a lemon
1⅓	*cups chicken broth or water*
½	*cup chopped fresh parsley*
	Salt and freshly ground pepper (to taste)

To peel the chestnuts, place in a small saucepan and cover with water. Bring to a boil, then remove the pan from the heat. Using a slotted spoon, remove the nuts one at a time and, with a paring knife, peel off both the shell and the inner skin. Discard any flesh that is moldy. Cut the chestnuts into small pieces and set aside.

Prepare the brussels sprouts by trimming the stem end if necessary and removing any unattractive outer leaves.

With a paring knife, make an ½-inch-deep slash across the stem end. Place the sprouts in a vegetable steamer and set aside.

Heat 1 tablespoon of the olive oil in a small (1½-quart) flameproof casserole or saucepan. Sauté the onion until soft, about 5 minutes. Add the bulgur and sauté briefly, stirring to coat all the grains. Add the chestnuts. Squeeze the half lemon over the bulgur (through a sieve) and stir once. Add the broth or water and bring to a boil. Cover the casserole, reduce the heat, and simmer (allow about 20 minutes from this point for the bulgur to cook completely).

Meanwhile, after the bulgur has been cooking for about 10 minutes, begin to steam the brussels sprouts. After 5 more minutes, check the bulgur (don't stir). It should be almost done and there should still be some liquid in the pan. Gently add more broth or water if necessary. Sprinkle the parsley over the bulgur. Replace the cover and continue to cook for 5 more minutes or until done. Meanwhile, check the brussels sprouts and remove them from the heat if they are done. When both the sprouts and bulgur are cooked, add the sprouts to the pilaf and toss with the remaining olive oil, salt, and pepper. Check the seasonings and serve hot.

Makes 4 to 6 servings.

Bulgur-Stuffed Zucchini

These summer-fresh stuffed zucchini can be baked in the oven or in a covered grill, if you like. Their flavor hints of the Aegean, with feta cheese, lemon, and thyme. Vary the vegetables as you wish, but don't eliminate the tomato.

1½   *cups cooked bulgur, at room temperature*
1   *small onion, chopped*
2   *scallions, chopped*
1   *medium tomato, diced*
1   *small red bell pepper, seeded and diced*
½   *cup fresh or frozen green peas*
½   *cup crumbled feta cheese*
¼   *cup chopped fresh parsley*
½   *teaspoon fresh thyme leaves*
      Salt and freshly ground black pepper (to taste)
      Juice of 1 lemon
      Approximately 2 tablespoons olive oil
3   *to 4 medium zucchini or other summer squash*

Preheat oven to 375°F.

In a bowl, combine everything but the lemon juice, olive oil, and zucchini and mix well. Slice the zucchini in half lengthwise. Gently scoop out the seeds and some of the pulp and discard or save to use at another time, leaving shells about ⅜-inch thick. Brush the insides of the shells with a little olive oil, and sprinkle with salt and pepper if desired. Spoon some of the bulgur mixture into each. Sprinkle lemon juice and olive oil over the filling.

Brush the bottom of a baking dish lightly with olive oil. Place the stuffed zucchini in the dish. Pour just enough water into the dish to be about ⅛-inch deep. Cover the dish with foil and bake in preheated oven until the zucchini is nearly tender, about 45 minutes. Remove the foil and continue to bake for another 10 minutes, until the filling begins to brown.

Alternately, place the stuffed zucchini on a lightly oiled vegetable rack that will fit into your grill; cover the grill and cook until tender, about 30 minutes.

Makes 4 servings.

Bulgur-Stuffed Zucchini (right) ready for grill or oven.

© Bill Milne

HOW TO SPROUT GRAINS

Sprouting your own whole grains is easy, economical, and guarantees freshness. Sprouted grains are rich in protein, fiber, and vitamin E; the smaller ones are wonderful added raw to salads or sandwiches, while the larger ones you will probably prefer to cook briefly or add to bread.

Depending on the size of the grain, sprouting takes from two to five days. Sprouts are tastiest when eaten fairly small, from one-eighth to one-half inch in length. Sprouting is done in the dark, but if you wish, you can "green" the shoots by leaving them in sunlight before you eat them. Sprouts are most flavorful the first two or three days after they are ready, but they will keep for about a week in the refrigerator and you can freeze them if you don't mind that they're limp when thawed. If you are really interested in different ways to use them, try drying your sprouts in a low-temperature oven and then grinding them into flour.

Two words of caution to ensure that your sprouts are as good for you as they look. First, just about any whole grain (groat or berry) that you buy can be sprouted, but you should avoid sprouting any that are intended as garden seed, as they may have been treated with pesticides or growth enhancers. Second, sprouts are one good thing that you can truly have too much of; if eaten in excessive amounts, they may initiate an autoimmune reaction similar to lupus. There is no likelihood of this if

Various stages of sprouting.

you are including sprouts as a recipe ingredient; you just don't want to choose them as a dietary mainstay.

All you need to sprout grains is water, a dark place (not the refrigerator), a separate jar (quart-size is usually appropriate) for each type of grain, a piece of cheesecloth to cover it, and a rubber band. Small grains like quinoa or amaranth can be sprouted on rustproof trays if you have the space to do so. You will need enough cheesecloth or paper towels to line and cover the trays.

Rinse the grains in a sieve and discard any that are broken or abnormal. Put them in a jar and cover with cold water—about four times as much as their volume. Cover the jar with cheese-

cloth secured by a rubber band. Let soak at room temperature for eight hours in warm weather; twelve in cold.

If any debris floats to the top of the water, remove the cheesecloth and spoon it out, then replace the cheesecloth. Drain off the water in the jar through the cheesecloth. Hold the jar under the tap and fill with fresh water. Swish the grains around and then drain off the water as before. (If the soaking water was particularly gelatinous, repeat this step.) Invert the jar in your sink or dish drainer for a few minutes to ensure that it drains thoroughly.

For large grains, turn the jar and shake it so the grains lie along one side. Put the jar in a dark place to begin sprouting. As explained above, rinse and drain the grains twice a day until they reach the desired size. Should they fail to sprout or an unpleasant odor develops, discard them.

For small grains, line a rustproof tray with damp cheesecloth or paper towels. Drain the soaked grains as explained above and spread them out over the cheesecloth. Cover with another damp cheesecloth and put in a dark place to begin sprouting. Check the tray twice a day and sprinkle water over the cloth to keep it damp.

If you wish to green your sprouts, leave the jar or uncovered tray in sunlight for about four hours once they have reached the desired size. Rinse thoroughly and refrigerate in an airtight container with a damp paper towel.

© Michael Grand

Bread baking is one of the most re-warding of all culinary skills. There is something elementally satisfying about the process, from watching the yeast send up its first frothy bubbles through kneading what seems to be an impossibly sticky mess until it turns into wonderful, smooth dough; from the al-ways surprising thrill of the first rising to the fabulous, comforting aroma of the baking loaves, to perhaps the ultimate exercise in self-restraint—trying not to

eat it all at once. The taste and nutri-tional value of bread baked at home far surpasses commercially baked and pack-aged loaves and rivals anything pro-duced by a small specialty bakery.

Bread baking is a skill, but it is not a difficult one to master. Here are a few things to keep in mind:

Attitude. Many factors contribute to a successful loaf of bread. The first thing to remember is that the process (at least in your kitchen) is not an exact science.

The ingredients, the weather, the oven, the pans, even your mood all play a slightly unpredictable role in the final product, so don't agonize over the pro-cess. Relax. Once you begin to get the hang of it, bread seems to happen—the failure rate is minimal.

Experience is the best teacher. It is true that practice makes perfect. It is possible to teach yourself to bake bread, but someone who is good at it can give you an invaluable head start. Much of the mystery of the process is really just knowing what it is supposed to look and feel like. If you can watch someone else bake bread before you try it on your own, you'll give your confidence a boost.

Begin with the basics. Your first efforts at bread baking should be with a recipe that uses mostly wheat flour, whether whole, white, or a mix. None of the other flours react with the yeast and liquid to rise as well as wheat, and therefore, you will have the most predictable results with it.

Busy people do have time to bake bread. Yes, it's true, bread takes quite a few hours to make, but it really only needs your attention for a small part of that preparation time. Unless you are making a terribly elaborate recipe, most bread can be mixed, kneaded, and set to rise in about half an hour. About one hour later, you'll need to spend another ten to fifteen minutes getting the dough into shape. Thirty to sixty minutes later, you'll have to put it in the oven. Then, in another thirty to sixty minutes, you'll have to take it out. That seems to total about forty-five minutes of actual work time, not bad at all when you consider the results. What you cannot do while you are making bread is leave the house for a long time or forget to keep an eye on the various risings. However, if you want to start ahead of time, bread dough can be refrigerated, or even frozen, before either of the rising periods. Be aware that even cold dough can have a mind of its own and some recipes will rise in the refrigerator, which may or may not be an asset. If you ever find that you have let the dough rise too much, just punch it down and let it rise again.

Understanding the Basics

In brief, bread is a mixture of flour, a leavening agent (usually yeast), and liquid (usually water or milk). It almost always contains a sweetener, which helps the yeast to grow, some salt, which helps to control the speed at which the yeast rises, and may contain oil or butter and eggs as well as myriad flavorings.

Yeast is a living microorganism. When it gets wet and warm, it activates the gluten in the flour and forms carbon dioxide bubbles that cause the dough to rise. Yeast is available in two forms: *compressed* and *active dry.* Compressed yeast comes in small cakes and must be kept refrigerated. It spoils very quickly and must always be tested before you add it to the other ingredients. Active dry yeast comes in small foil envelopes (you can also buy it in bulk at health-food stores), and has a fairly long shelf life. It is not necessary to test it before you add it to the other ingredients, but doing so is always reassuring. Both kinds of yeast are sold dated; do not buy them if the dates have passed. One cake of compressed yeast equals one packet of active dry yeast, or a scant tablespoon, and they can be used interchangeably, especially useful when you are running low on one or the other.

Gluten is two specific proteins. It is found primarily in wheat and to some extent in triticale and rye. Flours that do not contain gluten can be mixed with those that do; if used alone, they must be leavened with something other than yeast, usually baking powder or baking soda. Non-yeast-leavened baked goods are usually referred to as quick breads; they also include many pancakes, muffins, biscuits, cakes, cookies, and most other forms of pastry.

Flour makes the biggest contribution to the flavor of your bread. The kind of flour you choose also affects the texture and weight of the loaf. As you become accomplished at baking bread, you will learn to experiment with kinds and proportions of flours. You'll find that running out of a specified flour in the middle of a recipe is not the end of the world—using another kind may produce a loaf you like even better.

The *liquid* used in bread affects the texture of the loaf. Water is a very common choice. It will make a slightly coarser loaf than milk, which adds a velvety texture (as well as protein, calcium, cholesterol, and fat). You can experiment with a recipe by substituting one with the other or combining the two. You can also use beer, vegetable broth, or fruit juice; they will affect the flavor and color in obvious ways. Eggs add light, rich tenderness and a golden color to bread, and make the dough stickier.

Sweeteners help the yeast to grow, and most recipes call for at least a teaspoon. This small amount will not make the bread taste unduly sweet, but adding more will begin to influence the flavor. Molasses and honey will add color as well. Sweeteners should be added to the warm liquid when you first dissolve the yeast. Sweeteners also help bread to stay fresh.

Salt moderates the speed at which the dough rises. If you eliminate it completely from a recipe, the dough may rise faster than indicated. This may inhibit the full flavor development and create an uneven texture with large holes. If you are on a strict salt-free diet, leave the salt out of your dough, but be aware that it may behave a little differently. If you are just trying to cut down

on salt, you will probably be happier with the texture of your bread if you allow a half teaspoon of salt per loaf.

Fat contributes moisture to bread and prolongs freshness. It also helps to keep the bread from rising too quickly. Bread that contains no fat has an open texture and is chewy. Fat can be butter or margarine or a vegetable oil; the one you choose may or may not affect the flavor. Butter and olive oil, for instance, lend characteristic tastes, while that of safflower oil is insignificant.

The additional ingredients you find in bread recipes add flavor or zest. They can range from spices and herbs like caraway and dill to vegetables and fruits like onions and raisins. Adding these nonessentials can transform a basic recipe. Feel free to experiment. In general, herbs and spices or anything that will blend with the overall flavor should be added with the liquid or flours, and heavier ingredients such as raisins and nuts can go in at the second kneading. Your imagination can be the limit as far as what you add to a basic recipe. However, ingredients that contain their own liquid—like cottage cheese or applesauce—will almost certainly change the balance of the dough. It is best to follow a recipe that calls for these.

Digging In

Assemble your equipment first—your hands are going to be very sticky before you get too far. You'll need at least one measuring cup, a set of measuring spoons, one or two large, steady mixing bowls, a wooden spoon, a pastry board, some vegetable oil, a damp dish towel, and all the ingredients. In addition, a dough scraper is very handy for cleaning the board.

When you mix bread dough, your mixing bowls and all of your ingredients should be at room temperature, or warmer if the recipe so indicates. Yeast is sensitive to temperature. If it is too cold it will not grow, if it is too hot it may die. That said, it really takes extreme temperature to damage yeast.

To begin, you usually dissolve the yeast in warm liquid. Tap water that feels very warm but not hot on the inside of your wrist is about right for active dry yeast; a little cooler is correct for compressed. If the recipe calls for milk, warm or scald it and let it cool a bit; don't pour it steaming over the yeast. Let the yeast mixture sit for five or ten minutes before you add anything; it should begin to bubble, forming gooey-looking clouds on the surface of the liquid. If it fails to do so, don't waste ingredients or time on it as your bread will not rise; start over with fresh yeast.

It is not necessary to sift flour when making bread. However, nonwheat flours are sometimes lumpy. If so, sift or whisk them to be sure they will blend well. You will notice that many bread recipes call for approximate amounts of flour. This is because different flours (including different brands of the same kind of flour) absorb liquid differently; the humidity also affects this. It is really a matter of choice whether or not you blend all your flours together before adding them to the yeast and liquid. Doing so will ensure that your mix has the exact proportions called for, but if you don't need to use it all, you'll end up with an odd batch of flour (a good solution to this problem is to save any leftovers and use them for pancakes).

As you mix the bread, add flour until the dough holds together (it should form a ball that pulls away from the sides of the bowl as you stir), then turn it onto a floured pastry board and begin to knead it, working in more flour as necessary. Too much flour will make a heavy loaf, so it is better to be a little stingy with it before the first rising. If the dough seems too sticky after this, you can work in a little more flour.

Recipes usually instruct you to knead the dough until it is smooth and elastic. Kneading is the process of flattening and folding the dough that allows the gluten in the flour to be developed. Use both hands and press down on your ball of dough, then fold it back up over itself and press again. As you press and fold the dough, rotate in on the board so that you handle all parts of it equally. You will find that you develop a natural rhythm as you knead. If the dough sticks to the board, dust it with a bit more flour. If the dough sticks to your hands—particularly if there are eggs in it—try putting just a little oil on them.

When the dough has been kneaded enough, it really will turn smooth and elastic. It will form a firm (but not hard), spongy ball with a satiny surface that breaks into little air bubbles as you stretch it. It usually takes five to ten minutes of kneading to reach this stage.

At this point the dough should be placed in an oiled bowl to rise. (You can let it rest on the floured pastry board for a minute while you wash out your mixing bowl.) The oil helps the dough to climb up the sides of the bowl. When you put the ball of dough in the bowl, turn it over once to oil the top—this will keep it from drying out as it rises. Cover the bowl with a damp dish towel and put it in a warm place to rise. (A warm place can be near a radiator or heat vent, in front of a sunny window, or inside an oven that was preheated to warm and then turned off.)

While the dough is rising, clean any stray bits of dough off your pastry board (these will only be in the way for the next kneading). Then prepare the pans or trays that you wish to use.

Most bread can be baked either in a loaf (or other shape) pan or flat on a cookie sheet. But bear in mind that the sides of the pan give the dough a support to rise up. Bread that is baked on a cookie sheet is likely to spread as it rises, making a low but not necessarily heavy loaf. The recipe will tell you how to prepare the pans; they are almost always oiled and sometimes dusted with flour or cornmeal.

The dough should roughly double in size when it rises the first time. When it is ready, the depression made if you poke a finger into it will keep its shape. Try not to let the dough over-rise, as it wastes the yeast's energy.

Put the bowl next to your pastry board and punch down the dough by gently plunging your fist into it. Then gather it into a ball and put it on the board. Knead the dough again for a few minutes. This second kneading knocks the excess air out of the dough. In addition, it prevents large air pockets from forming in your bread.

If you let the dough rest for a few moments after the second kneading, you will find it easier to shape it into loaves. This is particularly helpful if you are planning to braid or roll it up over a filling. Cut it into the appropriate number of pieces and form each into the approximate shape you wish, then walk away for a few moments (the time it takes to wash the rising bowl). When you return

you'll find that the dough can be shaped without argument.

To shape dough for loaf pans, form into a rectangle about the length of the pan, flatten it, fold the two long edges together, and pinch to seal. Rotate the dough so this seam is on the bottom. Pinch the ends to seal and put the dough into the pan, tucking the ends under if it is too long.

To make a filled loaf, shape each portion into a rectangle about the length of the pan, then roll or stretch the piece in the other direction until it is about a half-inch thick. Spread it with the filling and then roll it up like a jelly roll. Pinch the edges to seal and place in the pan as described above.

To braid the dough, lightly roll the dough between your hands to make three log shapes (just like clay in grade school). After they have rested, you will be able to lift them and shift their weight from one end to the other, which will help to stretch them to the desired length. Place these side by side on the board and braid them, sealing the ends by tucking them under when you place the braid on the cookie sheet.

Cover the loaves with a damp towel and leave them to rise as before. The second rising does not usually take as long as the first, and the dough should not quite double in size. If you are letting the dough rise in your oven, be sure to take it out (gently) while you let the oven preheat.

Bake the bread as instructed in the recipe. Glass and ceramic pans retain more heat than metal ones; if you are using them you may want to lower your oven temperature 25°F from that specified. Bread baked on a cookie sheet will probably need less time than the

same recipe baked in pans, because it will not be as lofty a loaf. Bread is done when it pulls away from the sides of the pan and sounds hollow when tapped on the bottom. You have to remove it from the pans to do this; not all bread wants to be removed from the pans while it is hot, so don't fight it. (If you are really uncertain about its state, test it as you would a cake. This will mar the surface slightly, but you are going to cut it soon anyway.) If the bread seems to be browning too quickly, you can cover it loosely with a piece of aluminum foil.

Once the bread comes out of the oven, try to remove it from the pans as soon as possible. This will help the hot steam to escape and keep the side and bottom crusts from becoming soggy. If the bread is stuck to the pan, release the sides by running a thin spatula around them. Invert the pans and tap the bottoms. If the bread does not pop out, don't try to force it, but leave the pans on a wire cooling rack for about ten minutes and then try again.

Take a deep breath and force yourself to let the bread cool a bit before you cut it. If there is too much steam in the loaf when you slice it, the cut edge will condense and look glued together; if your loaf is a particularly light one, you could ruin its height completely by the force of the cut. Always let your bread cool completely before wrapping it.

Bread keeps best airtight at room temperature. Unless it is very hot and humid, there is probably no need to refrigerate it. If you do not plan to eat it within four or five days, you can freeze it (which actually keeps it fresh better than storing it in the refrigerator), then defrost at room temperature.

The flavor and shape possibilities for fresh, homemade pasta are virtually unlimited.

Pasta, the Italian term for the humble noodle, is as versatile a culinary basic as rice. Indeed, pasta has a distinctive place in many ethnic cuisines. Noodle dishes are commonly found in the cuisines of Asia and Eastern Europe and are as delicious as the more familiar ones of Italy—and one can't help loving classic American macaroni and cheese.

Pasta is an excellent source of carbohydrates and does not deserve its reputation as a fattening food. The essential ingredients of pasta are flour, water or eggs, and a little salt and oil. Pasta can be made with almost any type of flour, or a blend of several, and can be flavored with pureed vegetables, herbs, and spices. These extra ingredients will

alter the color of the dough as well as the flavor, making dishes that are attractive to the eye as well as the palate. Of course, pasta dough can be cut or extruded in many shapes, filled and sauced in endless ways, and used in salads, soups, casseroles, and even puddings.

Ready-made pasta is sold fresh, frozen, or dried. Although there is a certain cachet associated with fresh pasta, all types are good. Because they are particularly durable, some of the dried shapes made from durum or semolina flour are actually preferred for stuffing and baking or serving with chunky sauces. Many forms of pasta are readily available at the local grocery. Ethnic markets, health-food stores, and gourmet shops are good sources of the less usual types.

Pasta is easy to make; the process is not nearly as involved as bread baking. It can be fun to experiment with the different flours and seasonings and a delightful adventure to choose or invent the perfectly complementary topping or filling for your dough.

A word on ingredients: the classic dried pasta that you buy is usually made from durum wheat, which has a high gluten content and makes a very stiff dough. It is very difficult to work with and not recommended for the home cook. Use unbleached all-purpose flour and eggs to make classic noodles, use water instead of eggs to make *udon* or *soba* (Japanese noodles) or if you are on a cholesterol-free diet. Eggs contribute a delicate flavor and rich color, salt acts as a flavor enhancer, and olive (or other vegetable) oil will make the dough easier to handle.

There are six steps in the pasta-making process: mixing, kneading, resting, rolling, cutting, and drying. Just as in bread making, flour should be added gradually to accommodate variations in quality or humidity; kneading develops any gluten in the flour so that the dough will be elastic; resting lets the gluten relax so that the dough is manageable. Pasta can be mixed by hand or with a

food processor, and it can be kneaded, rolled, and cut by hand or with a pasta machine. In addition to the ingredients listed in your recipe, you will need a pastry board or marble work surface, a long rolling pin, a sharp knife, some plastic wrap, and a dish towel.

Mixing and Kneading

By hand: Sift most of the flour into a mound on the pastry board. Hollow out a well in the center. Add the eggs (or water) to the well with the salt and oil, if desired. Beat the egg mixture with a fork or your fingers, gradually combining it with the surrounding flour. To do this, support the outer walls of the mound with one hand while pushing flour from the edge of the well into the egg mixture with the other. Continue until all of the flour and liquid has been incorporated into a thick paste. Dust the pastry board with flour. Knead the dough with the heel of your hand, adding more flour if the dough is sticky. The dough should be stiffer than bread dough. Knead until it is silky, smooth, and elastic throughout, for approximately five to ten minutes.

With a food processor: Put the flour and salt into the bowl of your food processor. Using the steel blade, pulse several times to mix. Mix the eggs (or water) with a little oil in a measuring cup. (The oil will help process the dough more easily.) With the machine running, gradually pour the liquid through the feeding tube into the dry ingredients. Allow the processor to run until a ball of dough forms around the machine's central rod, about fifteen seconds. Turn the machine off, test the dough, and add more flour if it is too

sticky; process again for a few seconds. Place the dough on a floured pastry board and knead for about three minutes.

Kneading with a pasta machine: Mix the dough by one of the preceding methods, but do not knead it. Adjust the smooth rollers of your pasta machine to the widest setting and dust with flour. Pass one handful of the dough between the rollers. Fold the flattened dough into thirds or halves, rotate it ninety degrees, and pass it through the rollers again. If the dough seems too porous, dust it with flour before passing it through the machine again. Repeat the process up to ten times, until the dough is smooth and has no holes, but do not knead it any more than necessary. Knead the remainder of the dough in the same manner.

Resting

After kneading the dough, form it into a ball, or flour and stack the thick strips produced by your pasta machine. Wrap in plastic wrap and let the dough rest for one half to two hours. The longer you let it rest, the softer and easier to handle it will be.

Rolling

Note: If you plan to make filled pasta, read that section on page 109 before proceeding.

By hand: Dust the pastry board with flour. Place a ball of dough about the size of an orange in the center. Dust your rolling pin with flour. As you roll the dough into a circle, press away from your body more than down into the dough. Begin each stroke in the center of the circle and rotate the dough ninety degrees between strokes. When the circle is six to eight inches in diameter, rotate it 180 degrees between strokes and coax it into a rectangular strip. Dust the board with more flour as necessary.

When the sheet of dough is about a quarter-inch thick, roll the far end toward you onto the rolling pin. Roll and stretch the strip away from you, pressing and sliding your hands along the rolling pin and then letting the dough slide off the pin. (This broad pressure will ensure that each stroke widens as well as lengthens the dough.)

Continue rolling and stretching until the dough is so thin you can see the pastry board through it. Set the finished strip aside under a cloth. Roll out the remainder of the dough in the same manner; dust the finished sheets with flour and stack them loosely under the towel. Let them rest for about fifteen minutes.

With a pasta machine: Adjust the rollers on the machine to the second-widest opening, dust with flour, and run each sheet of dough once through the rollers lengthwise. Support the dough and feed it into the machine with one hand while you operate the rollers with the other. Stop the machine periodically and slide the most recently rolled portion of the dough out flat on the work surface; don't allow it to bunch up. Repeat the rolling process once on each progressively narrower setting of the rollers. The sheets of dough should increase in length only; if they become too long to handle easily, cut them in half.

The finished sheets of dough should be paper thin and twelve to eighteen inches long. Dust the sheets with flour and stack loosely under a dish towel. Let them rest for about fifteen minutes.

Cutting

By hand: Place the sheets of dough on the pastry board and use a sharp knife to cut them to the desired size and shape. Cut straight down without dragging the knife through the dough. You can use a fluted pastry wheel to give noodles a fancy edge, or a biscuit cutter to make rounds for stuffing. (You can also purchase special rollers and trays to shape ravioli.) To cut long thin pasta such as fettuccine, fold the strips into loose flat rolls and cut through all the layers at once. Cut lasagna and small shapes one layer at a time. Pile loosely and let rest for five to ten minutes before cooking.

With a pasta machine: Refer to your machine's manual and select the appropriate size of cutting rollers, then dust them with flour. Make sure the sheets of dough are no wider than the rollers. Support the dough and feed it into the machine with one hand while you operate the rollers with the other. Stop the machine periodically and slide the cut noodles out flat onto the work surface. Pile the cut pasta loosely and let it rest for five to ten minutes before cooking.

Drying

Dry pasta for long-term storage by hanging it on a pasta rack, clothesline, towel rack, or over the back of a chair, or heap it on a towel. Let it dry for about four hours, or longer if the weather is humid.

Storing Pasta

Dried pasta can be stored indefinitely in an airtight container in a cool, dry place. Fresh pasta can be refrigerated in an airtight container for five to seven days or frozen for up to a month.

Making Filled Pasta

The dough for filled pasta should not be rolled quite as thin as regular noodles and it should be cut and filled immediately after rolling. When making ravioli, you can roll the dough into a sheet, dot it regularly with filling, cover it with a second sheet of dough, and then cut it apart through the borders between the filled mounds. To make cannelloni or manicotti, cut the pasta, boil it for two to three minutes, drain, and place on a damp cloth to cool. Don't let the pieces touch or they will stick together.

Pasta fillings should be finely chopped or pureed so that they do not tear the noodles, and they should be well-drained so that the dough does not get soggy. Many fillings should be precooked, as they will not cook in the short time it takes to cook the dough.

When you add filling to the pasta, be sure to leave clean quarter-inch-deep borders at the edges; grease or stray filling will prevent the dough from sealing properly. To ensure a good seal, brush the edges with egg white or water before you press them together.

Freshly filled pasta tastes best when it is cooked no more than an hour after filling, but you can wrap it tightly and refrigerate for several days, or freeze it for up to a month.

Cooking Pasta

Most pasta tastes best when cooked al dente (a bit chewy). Fresh pasta cooks very quickly, while dried pasta cooks in less time than most packages indicate. When hot pasta is on your menu, put the water on to boil ahead of time, but don't cook the noodles until you are sure that everything else is ready.

Use a large pot and lots of water—at least four quarts per pound of pasta. Add salt if you like when the water reaches a rolling boil. A tablespoon of oil will keep the pasta from sticking together and the water from boiling over. Add the pasta to the boiling water in handfuls. Return the water to a boil as soon as possible (it's all right to cover the pot, but be sure to remove the cover as soon as the water reboils).

The boiling time will depend upon the size of the pasta, whether it is fresh, frozen, or dried, whether it is filled, and how long it takes to return the water to a boil. To be sure of perfectly cooked pasta, keep a close eye on it and test frequently. In general, fresh pasta cooks in one to eight minutes, filled pasta in five to twelve minutes, dried pasta in four to twenty minutes. Drain the pasta in a large colander as soon as it is done. Do not rinse it in cold water unless you plan to use it in a cold salad. If you are not going to add the sauce to the pasta immediately, put the hot noodles in an oiled bowl and toss them with oil so that they do not stick together.

Baked pasta dishes such as manicotti or lasagna are usually made with pasta that has been precooked for about one third of its normal boiling time. These dishes are then baked in a 350°F oven for ten to twenty-five minutes, depending upon their density and the nature of their fillings.

A few basic sauce recipes follow the pasta dough recipes below. The buckwheat pasta is traditionally used in Japanese cuisine; try it with any soy-based sauce. You can toss it with soy sauce and fresh-grated ginger. Or see the recipe on page 112.

Classic Egg Pasta

3   *cups all-purpose flour*
4   *eggs*
1   *teaspoon salt (optional)*
1   *tablespoon olive oil (optional)*

Make the pasta as described above.

Makes about 1 pound of dough, enough to feed 4 to 6 people as a main course or 6 to 8 as an appetizer.

Variations:
Prepare these variations as described above unless otherwise noted.

Eggless Pasta

3   *cups all-purpose flour*
¾ *cup water*
5   *tablespoons olive oil*

A mix of Classic Egg, Spinach, and Tomato Pastas in a light herb sauce.

Spinach Pasta

½ pound fresh spinach, cleaned
     *Ingredients for Classic Egg Pasta, less
     1 egg*

Cook the spinach and drain thoroughly, then pat dry and puree. Add to the flour with the eggs.

Tomato Pasta

4 *tablespoons tomato paste
     Ingredients for Classic Egg Pasta, less
     1 egg*

Add the tomato paste to the flour with the eggs.

Herb Pasta

6 *tablespoons fresh herbs: basil,
     coriander, dill, parsley, chives,
     tarragon, oregano, thyme, et cetera
     Grated rind of one lemon (optional)
     Ingredients for Classic Egg Pasta*

Chop the herbs finely, mash in a mortar, and stir in the lemon rind. Add to the flour with the eggs.

Whole Wheat Pasta

2 *cups whole wheat flour
     Ingredients for Classic Egg Pasta, less
     1½ cups all-purpose flour*

Set aside ½ cup all-purpose flour. Mix the remaining flours and make the pasta; add in more all-purpose flour if the dough is too sticky.

© Burke/Triolo

Buckwheat or Quinoa Pasta

1½ *cups buckwheat or quinoa flour
      Ingredients for Classic Egg Pasta, less
      1 cup all-purpose flour*

Set aside ½ cup all-purpose flour. Mix the remaining flours and make the pasta; add in more all-purpose flour if the dough is too sticky.

***Chinese Egg Noodles (above), tossed
with shrimp, bean sprouts, and lemon
grass.***

Chinese Egg Noodles

3 *cups all-purpose flour*
1 *teaspoon salt*
2 *eggs*
½ *cup water*
¼ *teaspoon sesame oil*

Mix the flour with the salt. Mix the eggs and water with the dry ingredients. After kneading the dough, form into a ball and smooth the sesame oil over the surface. Allow the dough to rest for 1 hour. Roll the dough out in sheets ⅟₁₆- to ⅛-inch thick and cut in strips ⅟₁₆- to ⅛-inch wide, or as desired.
Note: This dough can be used to make wontons or egg-roll wrappers.

Japanese Udon

3 cups all-purpose flour
1 teaspoon salt
1 cup water (or as necessary)

Mix the flour with the salt. Add ⅔ cup of the water to the flour and mix to make a ball; add more water if necessary. Knead the dough for 10 minutes and allow to rest for 1 hour. Roll the dough into sheets ⅛-inch thick. Cut into strips ¼-inch wide.

Japanese Soba (Eggless Buckwheat Noodles)

1½ cups buckwheat flour
2 cups all-purpose flour
1¼ cups water

Set aside ½ cup all-purpose flour. Mix the remaining flours and make the dough as for Japanese Udon; add in more all-purpose flour if the dough is too sticky. Roll and cut into thin noodles.

Oil and Garlic Sauce

The simplest garnish of all for pasta requires no cooking. Simply toss the hot noodles with olive oil, minced garlic, herbs, and salt and pepper to taste and sprinkle with Parmesan cheese. For something a bit more complex, try the following.

¼ cup olive oil
1 clove garlic, peeled and minced
5 sun-dried tomatoes, blanched and chopped
   Pinch of fresh herbs (to taste)
1 can tuna fish, drained (optional)
¼ cup dry white wine or chicken stock
   Salt and freshly ground pepper (to taste)
   Parmesan cheese

Heat the oil in a heavy saucepan over medium-low heat and sauté the garlic for about 2 minutes. Add the remaining ingredients, except the cheese, in the order listed. Cover the pan and heat through, stirring occasionally. Toss the sauce with the hot pasta or serve on top of each portion; sprinkle with Parmesan cheese.

Makes 2 to 3 servings.

This soba and udon salad is light, healthy, and easy to make.

Classic Tomato Sauce

Use this as a base for almost any pasta dish. You can vary the seasonings as you wish—try adding oregano, thyme, or tarragon, or sautéed mushrooms, or sliced, pitted black olives. You can also leave out the carrot and celery and puree the entire batch of sauce with ¾ cup of heavy cream.

2 *tablespoons olive oil*
1 *onion, peeled and chopped*
2 *cloves garlic, peeled and minced*
2 *stalks celery, chopped*
1 *carrot, peeled and chopped*
2 *pounds fresh tomatoes or 1 28-ounce can plum tomatoes*
    Salt and freshly ground pepper (to taste)
¼ *cup chopped fresh basil*

Heat the oil in a heavy saucepan over medium heat and sauté the onion, garlic, celery, and carrot until the onion is transparent, about 5 minutes.

If using fresh tomatoes, peel by dipping in boiling water for 30 seconds and slipping off the skins. Cut off the stem ends and squeeze out the seeds. If using canned tomatoes, drain and reserve the liquid. Chop the tomatoes and add to the sautéed ingredients. Bring the mixture to a boil, reduce the heat, and simmer the sauce, uncovered, until it thickens, 30 to 40 minutes. Stir occasionally and add the reserved tomato juice or a bit of water if it seems too thick.

Puree half of the sauce, then return to the pan. Add more liquid if necessary. Stir in the basil and season with salt and pepper.

Makes about 4 cups.

Classic Meat Sauce

2 *tablespoons olive oil*
1 *onion, peeled and minced*
2 *cloves garlic, peeled and minced*
½ *cup sliced mushrooms*
1 *green bell pepper, cored, seeded, and chopped*
1 *pound lean ground beef*
2 *pounds fresh tomatoes or 1 28-ounce can plum tomatoes*
½ *cup dry red wine*
1 *bay leaf*
1 *teaspoon fresh oregano leaves*
    Salt and freshly ground black pepper (to taste)

Heat the oil in a heavy saucepan over medium heat and sauté the onion, garlic, mushrooms, and bell pepper for 10 minutes. Add the meat and cook, stirring constantly, until the meat is no longer pink.

If you are using fresh tomatoes, peel them by dipping in boiling water for 30 seconds and slipping off the skins. Cut off the stem ends and squeeze out the seeds. If you are using canned tomatoes, drain and reserve the liquid. Chop the tomatoes and add to the sautéed vegetables and meat. Add the wine and seasonings. Bring the sauce to a boil, cover the pan, reduce the heat, and simmer, stirring occasionally, until it thickens slightly, about 1½ hours.

Makes about 6 cups.

Classic Cheese Filling

This simplest of fillings works well with any of the basic sauces.

1 *pound ricotta cheese*
½ *cup coarsely grated fresh mozzarella cheese*
½ *cup grated Parmesan cheese*
1 *egg*
2 *tablespoons chopped fresh parsley*
    Salt and freshly ground pepper (to taste)

Combine all the ingredients in a bowl and mix well.

Makes enough to fill pasta for 4 to 6 people.

Stir-fries are the Oriental version of pilaf. They begin with cooked grains and can contain almost anything else you wish. The ingredients must all be cut into very small pieces so that they cook quickly. They are added to the pan in the order of their cooking times and sautéed as necessary, then a small amount of seasoned sauce is added and the pan is covered and allowed to steam for a few minutes. Serve stir-fries sprinkled with toasted sesame seeds if you wish. The most successful stir-fries are made in a wok, but a large, well-seasoned skillet with a cover will also do.

Here is a sample recipe; vary the ingredients as you wish. Have everything ready to go before you start to cook.

Classic Stir-Fry

For the sauce:

¼ cup broth
  Grated rind and juice of 1 lemon
2 tablespoons soy sauce
3 tablespoons vegetable oil
1 scallion, thinly sliced (including green part)
1 inch fresh gingerroot, peeled and grated or thinly sliced
1 clove garlic, peeled and minced

For the stir-fry:

2 tablespoons vegetable oil (preferably part Oriental sesame oil)
1 tablespoon garlic, peeled and minced
½ teaspoon hot red pepper flakes (optional)
1 cup broccoli florets, thinly sliced
1 carrot, peeled and thinly sliced
1 cup mushrooms, cleaned and sliced
1 cup cabbage or bok choy, thinly sliced
2 cups cooked grain of your choice
6 scallions, finely sliced (including some of the green part)
1 bunch fresh spinach or watercress, washed and dried, and the tough stems removed

Mix together the ingredients for the sauce and set aside.

Heat the oil in a wok or skillet over medium-high heat. Add the garlic and red pepper flakes and sauté for 30 seconds. Add the broccoli and sauté for 2 minutes, stirring constantly. Add the carrot, mushrooms, and cabbage or bok choy and sauté for 2 minutes. Stir in the grain. Stir in the scallions and spinach or watercress. Stir in the sauce, cover the pan, reduce the heat, and cook until heated through, 3 to 5 minutes.

Soba Noodle Variation:

Substitute soba noodles for the grain. Cook them al dente while you are making the stir-fry. Drain and return them to the cooking pan with the prepared sauce. Toss to coat well, then add to the stir-fry. Toss gently and finish cooking as directed above.

There is nothing easier to make than your own granola—in fact, the most taxing part will be assembling the ingredients. Homemade granola need not be as rich or sweet as the packaged varieties, and you can use butter, margarine, or vegetable oil as you prefer. It keeps well if stored in an airtight container.

Granola

The ingredients in this basic recipe can be varied as you wish.

¼   *cup vegetable oil, margarine, or butter*

½   *cup honey*

6   *to **7** cups dry ingredients, including at least 3 to 4 cups rolled oats, wheat, or rye; and shredded coconut, sesame seeds, sunflower seeds, wheat germ, peanuts, almonds, cooked grain such as amaranth or kasha, and raisins or other (chopped) dried fruit*

Preheat oven to 350°F.

Whisk the oil and honey together (melt the butter or margarine if using). Chop or smash any nuts you are using. Mix together all the dry ingredients except the raisins or dried fruit in a large, oiled baking pan. Pour the oil and honey mixture over them and mix well. Bake in preheated oven for 15 to 20 minutes, stirring often. When the mixture is golden brown, remove from the oven, stir in the raisins, and allow to cool completely. Store in jars or plastic bags.

Makes 6 to 7 cups.

© Lynn Karlin

Homemade Granola (left) can be made with any of your favorite grains; it is so simple to mix that a child can "take charge" as long as you keep an eye on the oven.

PROP CREDITS

page 15—Amaranth Chicken Oriental:
plate, bowl, and cup courtesy
Platypus

page 19—Barley Flour Pecan Scones: background ceramic pitcher courtesy
Zona

page 20—Barley Pilaf with Mushrooms and
Dill: table courtesy ABC Antiques

page 25—Kasha Varnishkas: plate, fork, and
napkin courtesy Pottery Barn

page 28—Kasha Pilaf with Broccoli and
Mushrooms/Buckwheat Flour
Skillet Bread: plates and cup courtesy Platypus; candle holders
courtesy Pottery Barn

page 34—Corn Polenta Pasticciata: plate,
glass, and jars courtesy Pottery
Barn; wooden bowl courtesy Zona

page 40—Millet Pilaf with Shrimp, Fish,
and Zucchini: plate courtesy
Platypus; vases and spoon courtesy Zona

page 55—Quinoa Watercress Salad: plate
courtesy Platypus; pear candles,
gold wooden tray, and fork courtesy Zona

page 56—Quinoa Vegetable Skillet Cake:
copper pot and dried lavender
courtesy Zona; blue glass courtesy
Pottery Barn

page 64—Wild Rice Salad with Raspberry
Vinaigrette: raspberry-colored
plate courtesy Platypus; soapstone
plate and cruet courtesy Pottery
Barn; fork courtesy Zona; table
courtesy ABC Antiques

page 68—Basic Risotto: plate, bowl, and
cup courtesy Platypus; metal oak
leaves courtesy Pottery Barn

page 71—Simple Aromatic Basmati Pilaf or
Poultry Stuffing: fork courtesy
Platypus; table courtesy ABC
Antiques

page 79—Triticale and Black Beans: plate
courtesy Platypus; fork courtesy
Zona

page 81—Triticale Poultry Stuffing with
Lentils and Apples: ceramic verdigris apples courtesy Zona

page 90—Pizette: black marble cheese
board courtesy Pottery Barn

Zona: 97 Greene Street, NYC 212-925-6750

ABC Antiques: 888 Broadway, NYC
    212-473-3000

Pottery Barn: 700 Broadway, NYC
    212-505-6377

Platypus: 128 Spring Street, NYC
    212-219-3919